"YOU WANDER AROUND, SLEEP IN THE PARK OR AN OLD CAR, OR TRY TO FIND A CRASH PAD. YOU GET HUNGRY AND THEN HAVE TO BEG. YOU DON'T FIND THE LOVE YOU'RE LOOKING FOR. WHAT YOU DO FIND ARE SUBSTITUTES. SEX BECOMES THE FIRST AT-TRACTION . . . THEN YOU TRY MARIJUA-NA. . . ."

This is a young girl speaking—one of the many voices in this book. All have their own stories—the lost and desperately searching young people on the far-out side of the generation gap.

You may be shocked or even angered by the revelations here. But you will also be enlightened —and inspired by how David Wilkerson has shown so many young people that the greatest "trip" of all is into the grace of God.

# purple violet squish

# David Wilkerson

**ZONDERVAN BOOKS**
**Grand Rapids, Michigan**

All quotations from the Bible in this volume (unless otherwise noted) are from the Revised Standard Version of the Bible, copyright 1946 and 1952 by the Division of Christian Education of the National Council of Churches in the United States of America. Used by special permission.

**PURPLE VIOLET SQUISH**

A ZONDERVAN BOOK
Published by Pyramid Publications for Zondervan Publishing House

Zondervan Publishing House edition published 1969
Paperback edition published November, 1970
  Fourth Printing April, 1972

Library of Congress catalog card number: 79-81055

Printed in the United States of America

ZONDERVAN BOOKS are published by Zondervan Publishing House, 1415 Lake Drive, S.E., Grand Rapids, Michigan 49506, U.S.A.

purple~violet~squish

# introduction

Hippies
beads
buttons
bells
baubles
boots
tights
tassels
trips
teens
tawdry
terrified
weird
confused.

Hotly
pursuing
their
souls,
I
asked
one
question.
What
does
God
mean
to
you?

The girl,
painted
toes,
battered
suitcase
and
clutching
demon
paintings,
slithered
away
in
loquacious
silence.

The
harmonica
player,
breathing
out
a
dirge,
stunned
me—
GOD
IS
PURPLE
VIOLET
SQUISH.

The runaway,
black
robe,
dog bone
neck piece,
the devil
in
his
eyes,
whispered,
God
faded
away,
man.

# contents

# the hippies

# 1. the hippies

> "Every life is many days, day after day. We walk through ourselves, meeting robbers, ghosts, giants, old men, young men, wives, widows, brothers-in-law. But always meeting ourselves." James Joyce—*Ulysses*

*a sixteen-year-old girl tells me how it is*

"I ran away because I was depressed. In school everything seemed to be caving in on me. My parents thought I was hopeless. There was no love in the house at all. My father had a lot of money and could buy me anything but I wasn't very hung up on material things. One night after dinner we had an argument. The next day I packed up a few things and left. I went out in search of love.

"I went to Haight Ashbury. In no time I was broke and too ashamed to go home. Unless you know someone, you have no place to stay. You wander around, sleep in the park or an old car, or try to find a crash pad. You get hungry and then have to beg for money. You don't find the love you're looking for. What you do find are substitutes.

"Sex becomes the first attraction. But once you get involved there's nothing but guilt and shame.

13

"Then you try marijuana and soon the novelty wears off. The kids tell you about acid and speed and you are likely to try them. You come here just mixed up but soon you get weird. You start having hallucinations and your mind becomes unstablized for long periods of time. Your whole personality changes and you don't care about anything. You seem to melt into the universe. Drugs become your cause. Your life begins to revolve around them and they lead to the philosophies of mind expansion, cosmic consciousness, astrology and reincarnation. When you try to understand what's happening, you can't.

"Most trips on LSD are bad. Usually you experience manifestations of the devil and you feel you could actually lose your soul. I now know that articles in magazines like, 'I found God Under Acid' are the devil's lie, and that acid is a big counterfeit.

"I started grooving with Meth pills and dropping speed. I became a speed freak and never wanted to come down. I got so bad that once I even tried to shoot instant coffee in my veins.

"Kids don't realize it but you start turning on in degrees. When I first started taking acid I thought I was doing it to find out about myself but the opposite happened—I couldn't even talk to people anymore.

"Generally, a girl is accepted by the hippies here if she is ready to get pregnant, V.D., raped or beaten up. Then she is in because that is just what happens. I was raped once. I had a boyfriend who almost killed me with a knife.

"The hard drug pushers are moving in and trying

to turn on the hippies with heroin and cocaine. Pimps are trying to make the hippie girls their prostitutes.

"You come here to find love but you never will. I've burned all my bridges behind me. How very much I wish I could go back!"

*three kinds of hippies*

Bishop James Pike said of hippies: "There is something about the temper and quality of these people, a gentleness, a quietness, and interest—something good."

But try to tell that to thousands of deeply worried parents searching for their runaway kids. Thousands of teenagers are "splitting out" in search of the "superzap" love promised by hippies. I have found three classes of hippies in my travels around the world.

First there are the teenagers between fifteen and eighteen whom I call "hope-to-be" hippies. They are attracted primarily by the glamor and the mystique of the abandoned free life without the strictures of parents and the pressures of having to produce in the straight world. These teenagers confess to being tied up in knots: fear of sex, the draft, the threat of global nuclear suicide—all problems forced on them by the establishment. One "hope-to-be" explained it like this: "There's a river flowing today inside kids and you must ride with the flow until you reach the source. Once you find the source you flow out that river again into the world understanding true values."

The second group of hippies ranger in age from

seventeen to twenty-five and I call them "tribal" hippies. They have about them a sense of destiny and are hooked on drugs mostly for kicks. They are gripped by convictions of conspiracy and led by the logic of madness. Claiming they are on a search for God, they use drugs as a part of a charismatic religious experience.

Rejecting orthodox religion, they live by their own code. 1) Do your own thing. Be groovy and do whatever you want, whenever you want. 2) Get out of society. Cut the cord. 3) Shock the square community by wearing outlandish clothes and affecting unconventional mannerisms.

This group includes those who simply want to try something new and experiment with life. In a tribal kind of togetherness, they seek to shake off their terrible feelings of emptiness and to satisfy an inner craving for love and understanding.

The third group of hippies I call the "synthetic" hippies. Among them are the city hippies, the suburban hippies, poetical hippies, weekend hippies, musical hippies, Polynesian hippies and tourist hippies. They want the world to think they're hippies, but in their hearts they don't have the courage or the foolhardiness to go all the way. You see them in Greenwich Village and elsewhere on Friday, Saturday and Sunday nights, but they return to the straight world the rest of the week and carry on respectable careers.

Most in this group are about twenty-five years of age but some of them are in their sixties. Among them are business people who get a great kick out of rubbing shoulders with raw people. "Groovy cats" on weekend, they nevertheless think of themselves in terms of respectability and stability the rest of the time.

*a search for love and truth*

Love is the religion of the hippie. It is the "bag" of the new breed. Yet, in Haight Ashbury hippies told me that most of them have grown greedy because everyone is taking and no one is giving. They left the rat race because it was full of selfish people grabbing the cheese of materialistic success. Their own capitalists are now walking the streets selling underground newspapers trying to put "bread" money together.

Hippies claim they are looking for truth. But they are searching in the wrong places. No hunter goes out to sea in search of rabbits. It would be ludicrous for a fisherman to cast for trout on the desert. Hippies will discover themselves, find genuine love and comprehend the truth that sets men free, only as they relate their lives to God's love and His Son Jesus who fought the establishment all the way to the cross!

"Hip" is associated with being cool, far out and beat. The beatnik of the 1950's is the hippie of the 1960's. A hippie is one who removes himself from physical and intellectual reality. He believes only in himself, is extremely cynical and dislikes permanent relationships. He is obsessed by the futility and mediocrity of modern life. Most hippies have a strong psychological death urge. Their key word is "cool."

Some hippies seem to enjoy their way of life because of the great shock value it has for conventional society. One young hippie explained it this way. "At first you let yourself down into this world on a rope, hand-over-hand, looking down over your shoulder for a place for your feet. You are attracted by curiosity, but then you start looking for action. You come because the hippies are your idols and you are willing to exchange your mod fashions for hippie clothing. But it doesn't take long until you get confused and foggy in your mind and then you turn to drugs to clear away the cobwebs and try to get to know yourself better."

When you accuse the young hippie of dropping out on life and forgetting his responsibilities he will likely tell you that the first century prophet, Jesus Christ, was also a "groovy cat" who dropped out. He will try to sell you on the idea that Buddha and Saint Francis of Assisi were also dropouts who left their families to live in poverty.

What is the message that is attracting so many of our teenagers today? It is simply this. Whatever you want to do—do it without guilt. The only important thing in life is to feel good. Stay groovy and learn how to experience thrills. This bogus gospel is as old as the devil himself, but it is preached as a new doctrine. It is easily believed in a time of great moral landslide.

*hippies and narcotics*

Narcotics are an integral part of the hippie scene. I believe that marijuana started this whole pipedream that is a part of the unreality that permeates the hippie cult. Most hippies now take LSD, STP or other psychedelics. *The Random*

*House Dictionary of the English Language* defines psychedelic:

> Noting a mental state of great calm, intensely pleasurable, perception of the senses, esthetic entrancement, and creative impetus of or noting any of the group of drugs producing this effect.

LSD is a colorless, odorless, tasteless synthetic drug: de-lysergic acid diethylamide tartrate, compounded from an element of a rye fungus known as ergot. It was first discovered and produced in 1938 by a Dr. Albert Hoffman who worked as a chemist in a pharmaceutical firm in Switzerland. The curious power of the drug was not really known until 1943 when the chemist accidentally inhaled a small amount. LSD at one time was taken orally through sugar cubes saturated with the drug. It is now taken in pill form and produces distortions and hallucinations that defy description.

A single gram of LSD can provide up to two thousand doses, each dose capable of producing a "cop-out" experience lasting twelve hours or longer. The real danger of LSD is that it sets off a chemical reaction that continues long after the drug is no longer in the system. The "turning on" process is actually a short circuit of the sensory system. In medical terminology it is called "synesthesia."

LSD is not considered physiologically addicting. But say what they will, I have worked with many LSD users who were "hooked."

It was popularized in the United States in 1963 by two professors, Doctors Timothy Leary and

Richard Alpert of Harvard University. They lost their jobs after they involved theological students in reckless experiments with LSD, using divinity students as guinea pigs.

Dr. Leary went on to become the leader of the psychedelic movement and he now carries his "revival" to campuses in cities across the country. His followers include students, intellectuals, liberal ministers, professional people and a crazy collection of bearded prophets and gurus. I have followed Leary on college campuses in my lecture tours and have personally seen the widespread havoc that has resulted from his speeches and lectures. This "short circuit" prophet of the psychedelic movement believes that all reality is an abstraction. How he can sell this on any campus is beyond my comprehension! It is a known fact that after one of his appearances students produced their own LSD. How can such wild men be turned loose upon our young people to preach such damnable foolishness?

The frightening results of a bad trip can be tragic. At a hippie party in a western city a young college student, under the influence of LSD, grabbed a live kitten and ate it raw. Later he said he ate it only because he felt an urgent need to experience something new.

On the West Coast, the daughter of a well-known airline executive doused her body with kerosene and ignited herself with a cigarette lighter. Her bad trip on LSD ended with grim death.

A young LSD user attended one of my meetings in San Francisco. He stayed away from LSD for two weeks and on the first day of the third week, while sitting in chapel, he had a sudden epileptic-type seizure. He fell to the floor, bounced around on all fours and began barking like a dog. He grabbed the Bible and began to rip its pages. This delayed reaction is something we have witnessed among many of the LSD users who come to us for help. Some have had a chemical reaction even a year after their last trip.

I am even more concerned about the young users who have a good trip. They cannot see the danger and they are apt to return to the experience and keep at it until there is permanent brain damage.

LSD hippie cults are springing up all over the world. It has become a psychic revolt that even affects theology. Hippie "acid" heads and those involved with transcendental meditation have had visions of "God." Their descriptions are as bizarre as something from the devil's handbook. "God is a bare-chested creature with wings who carries a serpent entwined around a cross—a fire-breathing mountain who rises out from the earth spewing volcanos and spraying rainbows across the universe—a brilliant red ball of fire bathed in blue fog with a single eye that pierces your heart and makes it explode into millions of pieces that float through eternity—a tunnel into a cosmos of suspended nothingness where colors and designs kiss the soul and eternal joy is pulling God apart at the seams with a cord that has no end."

I believe the LSD movement is headed down into the same dark cave where all the radical new theologians are hiding. When Dr. Thomas J. Altizer says, "God is dead," he is saying the very same thing that LSD and psychedelic cultists have been saying for the past three years.

I had a shocking conversation with four psychedelic ministers. They told me they "dropped acid" (took LSD) before they undertook Bible study. They were especially intrigued by their study of the book of Revelation under the influence of LSD. One said, "Man, what a blast—even the beasts came to life." Under the influence of psychedelics, this generation of hippies is questioning the old truths in the Bible concerning resurrection, redemption, immortality, atonement and the miracle-working power of God. They seek salvation in a pill.

LSD has shot blasts of oxygen on the smoldering embers of doubt and agnosticism among young people who are challenging the church to do as much for them as their psychedelics can do. They see churchmen turning most of their attention to ecumenicism, civil rights and politics. Meanwhile, hippies are left to find God through LSD pills and answers in the cosmic fireworks of their own minds.

These young people claim science has painted itself into a corner of uncertainty. They are rejecting both religion and science. In essence, they are saying to scientists and ministers, "You have failed us, you have not given us the answers that satisfy the innermost longing of our hearts. You are all phonies. Physician, heal thyself."

the yippies

# 2. the yippies

"Politics is but the common pulse-beat of which revolution is the fever spasm." (Wendell Phillips, speech 1853)

On October 27, 1967, Father Phil Berrigan, artist Tom Lewis and Dave Eberhardt, Secretary of the Baltimore Interfaith Peace Mission, doused Selective Service files in the Baltimore Customs House with blood, in the hope that such an action would awaken the Christian community. As blood oozed over the files, a Unitarian Minister, James Engel, handed out copies of *Good News for Modern Man*, a recently published New Testament, to the clerks in the draft office and announced to the world that the records had been "anointed."

Mark Rudd, the revolutionary at Columbia University, commenting on this "collar power" action said, "Anyone can take a building, but to walk in and deface draft records, well that takes courage."

This draft board "bleed-in" was only one bizarre action of the unique yippie movement, now raising its head on the American scene. Yippies represent the political arm of the overall hippie movement. They hope to establish a political machine that can captivate the imagination of all rebels.

25

The first "yip-in" was held in 1967 in New York
City when hoards of yippies overran Grand Central Station and began to yip like dogs. A newspaper columnist coined the term "yippies" in explaining their unusual action.

Two political action groups now call themselves yippies. One group is called "Youth International Progressive Party" and the other, "Youth Interested in Politics." They are the hard core, political activists who lead demonstrations around the world. Though many are Maoists, others are members of the new left, determined to overthrow the establishment.

Yippies have invaded campuses country-wide to incite trouble and riots. In an effort to create a society more to their liking, they are willing to challenge the entire political and social structure. In their ranks are knowledgeable writers, artists, philosophers, musicians and others with a burning desire for martydom.

Ministers and priests are frequently leaders of the yippie rebellion. In an effort to be involved, they became entangled. They have not learned the difference between relevance and righteousness. James Engel, the minister involved in the draft board "bleed-in," explained, "Our act of anointing the draft files was such a beautiful thing, pregnant with the Judeo-Christian tradition. Blood was used to mark the doors of the Israelites in Egypt, thereby saving them from slaughter. For the draft files to be anointed, heralds the coming of the Holy Spirit, bringing new life to a dying world."

While awaiting sentence, some six weeks after the trial, Father Berrigan and Tom Lewis met with seven others and set out for another draft board, this time in Catonsville, a suburb of Baltimore. On May 17, 1968, they seized six hundred 1A and "immediate inductee files," dumped them into wire baskets, took them outside and after soaking them with napalm, burned them and recited prayers over the flames. The men were quickly adjudged "dangerous to the community" and jailed.

Among the yippies are missionaries to Africa and Latin America who claim that the natives do not want their souls saved as much as they want the Americans to leave their country and end the support of oppressive political regimes. Father Thomas Melville and Sister Marianna Peter, members of the Roman Catholic Maryknoll order, founded the Christian Guerilla Front in Guatemala. They came upon the idea in an effort to ease oppression. "We are presenting people with Christian morality. Our Christian guerilla front is determined to bring about true Christianity which is not permitted in Guatemala." When Maryknoll superiors evicted the group, they returned to the United States to begin looking for Christian guerillas interested in what they called "action Christianity." They were not long in finding priests and ministers ready to become political activists. This was the group responsible for pouring blood on the files of the Selective Service offices.

Other members of the yippies are radicals like Stokely Carmichael, Rap Brown and the Black Panthers. They are "yipping" at the heels of the "bourgeois dog." They are playing a radical game called, "Can You Top This?"

The yippies are frequently sponsored by misguided liberals with noble sentiments. Few yippie organizations are short of funds.

"Yippies are revolutionaries," proclaimed Jerry Rubin, the former Berkeley student activist. "We have merged new left politics with the psychedelic lifestyle. Our lifestyle—acid, long hair, freaky clothes, pot, rock music, sex—is the revolution. Our very existence mocks America. The old order is dying. The Democratic party is dying. While it dies, we will celebrate the festival of life. We are the politics of the future." These revolutionists were propelled into the public eye by the mass media in 1968 when they invaded Chicago for the Democratic National Convention. Shortly after their arrival, the yippies announced they would put LSD in the city's water system. Authorities immediately guarded its entire water system. On August 23, in Civic Center, with advance notice to the press, yippies were to have nominated a pig for President of the United States. The pig escaped, but seven persons were arrested.

A number of churches in the Old Town area offered a welcome to the yippies, set up medical and other facilities. They also issued a leaflet of invitation titled, "Yippies, we love you."

Among the yippies at a Lincoln Park rally during the convention were more than 200 clergymen who had come to lead a peaceful sit-in to advocate "open park" for the yippies. Bobby Seale of the Black Panthers, told the crowd of 2,000 to "Pick up a crowbar or a piece." Many yippies are members of the SDS (Students for a Democratic Society) and some of their demonstration techniques have been borrowed from the Zengakuren, a Japanese student organization, especially the techniques of snake dancing. A favorite action of the yippies is the taunting of police with chants of, "Pig, pig, oink, oink, soo-ee, soo-ee." Another favorite is, "Two, four, six, eight, organized to smash the state."

The yippies would be more dangerous but for two undeniable facts. They cannot crystallize their ideas and they fight among themselves. Their own bitterness and rebellion is so deep and overwhelming, it often spills out against their own. Each yippie is a little dictator unto himself. But the yippies have proved there is a strong dissent in America against war. Their war protestors usually burn draft cards in emotion-packed rallies with hundreds looking on. However, most of it is talk. Only a handful of yippie war protestors are AWOL in Sweden. A few have deserted while on military leave in Tokyo or the Phillipines.

There are "charlatans" among the yippies who preach non-violence but carry on activities which lead to violence, destruction and death. Recently, there has been a marriage between "yippie power" and "black power." This new power structure seeks an acknowledgment that America is the most racist nation in the world. They assert all white society is bankrupt and needs a complete overhaul. To the moderate whites and blacks who ask the yippies to renounce their delusions and work within the system, their answer has always been no! The yippies take an inflexible position of self-righteousness and moral superiority.

The Berkeley campus in California has become known as a rest home for yippies and a staging area for their leftist commando tactics. I have preached to hippies and yippies on the Sproul Plaza Mall while dozens of advocates of assorted causes distributed mimeographed sheets advocating such diverse actions as the end of the war, and end to the capitalistic system, and social justice for the Hell's Angels, a motorcycle club. The situation at the Berkeley campus has deteriorated to the point that now even the yippies are distributing pamphlets demanding law and order. On July 15, 1968 leaflets were handed out by members of the University of California Local AFL-CIO Clerical and Professional Employees Union, stating, "There have been at least eight rapes of women employees on the campus, some of them at gunpoint. On the average there are two armed assaults and robberies per day." The University's public relations office issued a statement to the San Francisco *Chronicle* stating that ten men had been added to its police force.

The yippies cannot tell the direction they are going and yet they plan. Their revolution is being fired by a movement called the underground press. Four years ago there were four underground papers. By October, 1968, there were 111 of them and their circulation is said to run over two million. Bearded yippies can be found hawking them in major cities. These papers scream against war, against puritanical sex, and call for legalized marijuana and psychedelics. Indicative of the type of journalism employed by the underground press is the following:

Democrats attending the Chicago convention were handed copies of the underground newspaper RAT with the face of Vice President Humphrey pictured on a dart board with a bullseye. The photo accompanied a Tom Hayden article which began, "We are coming to Chicago to vomit on the 'politics of joy.' "

A review of underground papers revealed that the yippies were planning new political activities from coast to coast on high school and college campuses. These demonstrations were to be undertaken on the streets of the ghettos in front of the United Nations and foreign embassies. Delighted with their millions of dollars worth of free publicity in Chicago, the yippies conjured up great plans. They asked students around the country to close down colleges and universities and join an election strike. Polling booths were to be leafleted and picketed. Demonstrators were to gather at the candidates' headquarters to inject Viet Nam into any victory celebration.

All this strategy, it was argued, would provide an example for high school students, blacks and all workers—to struggle against their institutions, schools, ghettos, labor unions, bosses, draft boards and all other forms of domination. For all the planning, however, little was accomplished.

American yippies are attempting to contact radical students in Paris, Czechoslovakia, Japan, Germany, Greece, Spain and elsewhere. They desire to establish an image of international revolution and call the masses of oppressed people throughout the world "brothers and sisters." They identify with Ho-Chi-Minh, Patrice Lumumba and similar nationalist leaders.

The main tactic of the yippie is confrontation, a

notion taken from the writings of Mao Tse Tung. They are not really interested in initiating a dialogue with the people against whom they are demonstrating simply because they do not have an alternative program to offer. Their revolutionary fever is fed by the sight of their own blood and the violent behavior of the police.

A liberal university administrator was quoted as saying that he would rather deal with an avowed communist than with leaders of the yippies: "With commies, you can have a sensible meeting because you know exactly what they stand for. But, with the new leftists, there is no pattern of rational thought. It is needleism, pure and simple. They want to disrupt and destroy, but they give no discernible indication of viable alternatives; only chaos with the new left in charge."

The yippie movement in my opinion is run more on slogan power than anything else. They demonstrate, not because of what they want, but because of what they feel.

Though small in number now, the yippies are growing and coming on strong. Let us hope they will just keep on talking!

"In loyalty to their kind,
They cannot tolerate our minds
And in loyalty to our kind,
We cannot tolerate their obstruction."
The Jefferson Airplane (*Crown of Creation*)

# the freebie gypsies

# 3. the freebie gypsies

I give the fight up;
Let there be an end,
A privacy,
An obscene nook for me,
I want to be forgotten,
Even by God.

Browning *Paracelsus*

Reflections of a freebie gypsy:

"When all this started, brotherly love prevailed. Hippies would walk up to you on the street and hand you a piece of bread or a flower. But that soon vanished and everything has gotten real tight. A lot of the first hippies have moved out. Every day the street just gets worse. You just can't find God and love in Sodom and Gomorrah. You've got to go to the hills and mountains—that's where God is."

There is trouble in hippie land. Murders and trips to insanity have shattered even the hardest and they're moving out. When James (Groovy) Hutchinson and Linda Fitzpatrick were murdered in New York's East Village, almost immediately some three thousand sets of parents were desperately walking the streets or visiting police precincts with graduation snapshots of runaway kids. One Wisconsin couple stayed in an East Village hotel for eight days while they toured the joints looking

35

for their daughter, Annabelle. In final desperation, they advertised in an underground newspaper: "Annabelle, we love you. No need to hide. Call Mom and Dad, collect."

Annabelle and her hippie friends escaped to a commune in a quiet rural area. Dozens of these communes are springing up all over the United States, Canada, Mexico and even in Europe. I coined the term "freebie gypsy" in 1967 in an effort to describe their kind of life. Freebie suggests their style of living and raising funds. They panhandle—involve themselves in prostitution—peddle their arts and crafts from door to door—and make their rounds to wholesale houses trying to scrounge whatever they can to feed the commune. They are gypsies because they have no permanent homes and authorities often force them to move.

This movement started with the do-gooder group called the Diggers who originally provided free food and shelter for hippies who were stranded. The first freebie gypsy community was established in 1965 near Trinidad, Colorado. It is called "Drop City." A young painter from Kansas shared his vision with a student from the University of Colorado. Together they purchased six acres from a rancher for $450.00. Their first shelter was their own car—from which they graduated to a tarpaper shack and finally to the geodesic design which was pictured in *Life* Magazine. At that time, twenty-one men, women and children were living together, devoting themselves to writing, painting and scrounging for food and other contributions. They set up this community, they said, because they wanted "freedom for out bodies, and freedom for our social selves. We want to be good. Besides freedom for our social selves, we seek love."

Their multi-colored geodesic domes consisted of welded automobile tops salvaged from junk yards. One of the "buildings" was topped off in gold— the top from a Cadillac. A red river of rusty rain poured through crevices between the welded tops, but those who lived there didn't care. They sloshed around in foul water, cooked their meals and slept together unconcerned. The nearby townspeople considered them nothing but scroungers, garbage pickers and tramps.

The freebie gypsies see nothing wrong in using psychedelic drugs but they prefer to call these experiences "sacramental and charismatic." They have their own gurus and spiritual leaders and devil priests. Convinced that civilization in the West is dying, they find it hard to believe there are any sincere people left in the straight world. Money is deprecated by them as a tool of the establishment used to acquire power.

The philosophies of the freebie gypsies are closely related to the mysticism of the Orient. Their manner of life reflects much of the way of life experienced by the Hopi Indians who, they believe, lived a peaceful, happy life. Transcendental meditation abounds in these communes and Buddhist and Hindu beliefs are also embraced.

Freebie gypsy communes are supposed to be "hot beds for happiness." It is a seductive way of life and the whirlpool action it creates, sucks in thousands of teenagers. Most amazing to me is the fervor with which these young gypsies try to attract others into the commune.

These communities represent a strange world where followers are taught an ersatz love. Work in these communes is not a virtue. They share with one another; however, in spite of all the talk about love, they fight, are suspicious of each other and steal whatever is not tied down.

One freebie gypsy told me, "This commune way of life is not organized. We have little use for money and fancy clothes. We don't need cash and when we do we just panhandle. Some of us are able to sell our art. The idea behind what we are doing is really love. Each day is a new experiment with beauty and understanding. No one is forced to work but we try to keep our places clean. No one is ever turned away, because we're trying to establish a model community where life can be one big orgasm."

But consider the case of Cathy, the daughter of a well-known Washington, D.C. couple who became intrigued with the hippie way of life. She started to hang around Deer Park Circle in Washington and soon began "dropping acid" with new-found friends. Her restlessness made her believe that she was being trapped by society and she resented her mother telling her what to do. It was 8:00 o'clock one Saturday night when her new boy friend, Francis, told her, "I'm going to San Francisco."

"Why?"

"Because I'm sick of it all. I want to go and find out what's happening."

The idea excited her. She, too, was disillusioned and anyhow everyone was saying, "Go up there, it's really groovy. You always have a place to stay. Everyone takes care of you. It's warm out there."

So they hitchhiked, something she had never done before. In six days they arrived with no place to stay. Francis disappeared. Some hippies promised to take her in for a week but they stole two hundred dollars from her. She ran away from them and met a group of kids who said they needed a couple more people to help start a commune.

She went on to describe their life together. "It was really terrible. Everyone was at each other's throat. One boy was dealing heavily in speed and heroin. There were all types of kids in and around the house. We started to get up tight and so a couple of kids left. They couldn't stand it anymore. We were using 'grass' and expected the house to be 'busted.' We really didn't love each other—just tolerated each other. The whole business was like standing in front of a fog bank. There is only fog there and you can't see reality. Everyone talks about being 'hip' and they hallucinate but all they see are mirages. Life itself became a mirage."

Most of the freebie gypsies that I have interviewed are still children at heart. You can't convince them that their way of life is a "cop-out" or a silly way of existence. There are few intellectuals among them and the majority suffer from mental confusion. Most are immature people who have convinced themselves that this way of life is the only true path to finding meaning and purpose. Saints they are not—in spite of all their talk about love and non-violence. There is a tendency among them to assume a holier-than-thou attitude and to be critical of anyone who does not agree with them.

During a recent crusade in Houston, Texas, I went backstage to counsel a large group of young people who came seeking help. I arrived just in time to see a young freebie gypsy standing on a chair and waving his arms with evangelistic fervor and ranting, "You can't find God in Mr. Wilkerson's meeting here. God is up in the mountains. Come and join us—we're all going up to Montana to establish a place. God is up in the hills."

Just why do these runaways escape to the hills and mountains seeking peace and rest? Some claim they are trying to escape from "psychedelphia"—a slang name given to urban areas where narcotics are easily available. Also, I think many of them try to run because they're weary of the meaningless relationships they have established.

The freebie gypsy is a completely new breed of hippie. In a way, he is better off than his hippie friends who live in the city. Lately, there has been a tendency in the communes to shy away from drugs and substitute transcendental meditation. One hippie summed it up this way. "We have outgrown the hippies. We may even yet end up in the square world."

Better than half of the freebie gypsy communes now in existence have been established as church-related programs. Some of them are doing an excellent work and should be commended. They have developed an environment of rustic living that is attractive to many runaways. Also, there is a real friendliness on the part of the people and, for the most part, it is genuine. But the thing that concerns me is that there are many college and high school students who find this kind of life compelling and are unwittingly being sucked into the hippie way of life.

What about religion and the freebie gypsy commune? Each one has a different faith because they take a little bit from here and there, put it all together and come up with their own cafeteria-style religion. It alarms me that they have hippie ministers—many of them claiming to be evangelical, who preach a dangerous gospel. They tell freebies they can have marijuana, LSD and Jesus, too. They drop acid and profess to study the Bible while they are tripping. They peddle LSD and marijuana and try to justify this foolhardy action by telling the kids their experience can be "sacramental." I say these men are wolves in sheep's clothing. These bearded ministers dressed in their kooky clothes and love beads, ridicule the church and the establishment. They talk about a relevant gospel of involvement. They delight in shocking other ministers and "enlightening" teenagers.

I view with horror the damage they have caused. While many of these hippie ministers have been applauded by certain of the clergy, the whole scene fills me with alarm. They do not preach an overcoming Christian life and they certainly do not understand the meaning of the cross. When you talk to them about their hangups—their marijuana smoking—their LSD trips—they look you right in the eye and say, "Don't judge brother, don't judge." Behind them they leave a trail of ruined bodies, twisted minds and lost souls.

Everyone at sometime in his life has thought

about getting away from it all. Weak, lonely, restless teenagers can be attracted to the freebie gypsy life. To join them, just stop the world and get off!

the freakniks

# 4. the freakniks

> "If the pursuit of peace is both old and new, it is also both complicated and simple. It is complicated, where it has to do with people, and nothing in this universe baffles man as much as man himself."
>
> Adlai Stevenson

Here come the freakniks—suspended in a spirit world of oblivion! They search for God in the surrealistic cosmos of drugs and emptiness engulfs them.

A freaknik blows his mind with "meditative implosion." His "freakout" is a transcendental trip—a fraudulent spiritual pilgrimage.

Hold on to your mind and read the confessions of some of the freakniks who, led by drugs and false religions, have descended to the nirvana of nothingness. I reiterate these tragic words of youth, for no description of mine could more accurately depict their soul-searing experiences.

Seventeen-year old Carl told me:
"I was involved in the study of Hinduism and pursuing mystic experiences for a few years. After I started using drugs, I easily went into ecstatic states and trances. At a love-in, a spirit came over me and I lost complete control of my

body. This happened a number of times with spirits I had allowed to enter me. I wasn't aware of what was happening. All I knew was that it took me out of myself and that was where I wanted to be—out of myself."

Consider this chilling freaknik confession:
"When I was in Los Angeles and smoking pot, I was thrown into trances by radio programs produced by 'wizards' who used fantastic imagery and spellbinding language. Of course, while you're under drugs you don't have much willpower and can easily be thrown into trances by a more dominant personality. I know others were influenced by the program and in turn used the same type of language to put others into trances. We didn't know what was happening. We just thought it was kind of fascinating. I know now that it was an incredible trick of the devil."

Religious freakout often begins with the study of Yoga, Hinduism and Oriental Mysticism. A twenty-eight-year-old former seminarian told me this:

"Seminary was just a continuation of book learning. I was looking for a personal inner experience —a viable encounter with Christ. I got started in meditation. Finally I dropped out of school and began to study Hinduism. Life became dark and dismal, but I continued. Many times I meditated for whole weekends. I got to the point where I really believed in Hinduism, so I switched from being a Christian. After I had studied Hinduism for some time, I turned to drugs and having visions and hallucinations. I thought this was really the truth because I was now experiencing the kind of things I'd been studying. I started hallucinating myself as God. It was a very powerful delusion, but I didn't recognize it at the time. Then I began to fall apart. I went from job to job and from one side of the country to the other and wound up here in Haight Ashbury. At the time, I thought this whole drug movement and meditation were going to open a lot of people's minds to great new things. There are still many people who believe this. Actually, all this is a trick of the devil to keep young people so fascinated they don't care what they do with their lives. The drugs reduce your willpower and then spirits enter. I am now obsessed with suicide—a total freakout at 28!"

Meet Jerry Dobb, a nineteen-year-old Negro boy who traveled the tragic path through the meditation mysteries.

"I attended a Baptist Church, read the Bible and even won scripture quiz contests. I was seeking deep revelations and began to read books by Christians who were considered mystics. Then I read *The Psychedelic Experience* by Timothy Leary and *The Tibetan Book of the Dead*. What you really do in meditation is totally empty yourself and allow spirits to come in and literally take you on a trip. Then anything can happen. You can get as high on meditation as you can by dropping LSD. This mystic meditation built to the point where my reactions become very slow.

I was here, but my mind was floating outside my head somewhere. I would write poetry and just say all kinds of things. I thought that what I was saying was beautiful, but in reality I was just talking in circles and it was plain foolishness. My whole sense of values and standards changed. I became a pessimist, resentful and full of hate."

How does a young runaway get involved in mystical freakism? One of their young converts told it like this:

"In some ways my life was a success but there was something missing. While I was searching, I came here one night to hear the swami speak and I was impressed. He was an old man, knowledgeable and at peace with himself. He was full of bliss and joy. I wanted to be like this.

I began to attend his meetings regularly and started to chant with others at the temple. I didn't chant at home at first, because I felt self-conscious. The swami told me it was necessary to participate in the chanting process. I couldn't make much sense out of it, and I didn't understand the philosophy. But gradually, as I kept chanting I found perfection of life. Now the difficulties and the miseries of life don't bother me. When I chant it is sacrificing my energies to glorify the supreme personality. That's why I now feel joy and bliss. This is transcendental pleasure as opposed to material pleasure. This is giving up yourself as an offering to Krishna, a pure spirit soul. The swami taught me that Christ was like a Buddha. Buddha and Christ have had time to deal with problems. Now it is time for Krishna."

One of the most fantastic freakouts is a result of playing the psychedelic game called "Allah-eye" during which two people gaze into each other's eyes trying to create a "God consciousness." They claim that you can see God if you look long and deep enough. Thomas Allan, a seventeen-year-old runaway from the Midwest, told me this frightening experience:

"I used to live with a girl who took a certain kind of drug which would dilate her pupils. When my eyes would meet hers I felt a strange sensation through me. My eyes would meet hers and it was like something or someone flashing a light into my eyes, except it wasn't bright, it was like electricity, like a power. This force was moving in on me and I couldn't turn my eyes away. I couldn't move my head. It caused this terrific cold fear to break out over my whole body. It was a colorful, spiritual force that moved through her and I felt I opened myself and for months I was in her power. A spirit of domination would throw us both into a trance and hold us. When the power weakened, we looked into each other's eyes again. We got to feeling guilty. She knew, when she stared at me something was going on. It was part of spirit domination. I knew that something had come upon me that made me helpless to deal with a superior power. You say to yourself—I don't really know what's happening. You subject yourself and allow the spirit to usurp your willpower. Satan was actually breathing on me and I could feel it through my whole body. I knew I was susceptible because my willpower was so weak due to drugs, that I actually wanted to be led by the nose."

This demon-possessed, freaknik religion is damaging the minds and damning the souls of American youth. And as I write this, the following invitation to what could lead to a country-wide freakout is appearing in three national magazines!

Take your mind on a vacation
STARSIN—CATARIAS
The 100% Legal High.

Why hassle with the exaggerated expense and legal hangups of pot when you and yours can enjoy equal rapture with a natural, legal and (as a result) much less costly, but equally effective substitute. STARSIN—CATARIAS is a dried derivative of the little known African shrub Nepeta—catarias, and can be smoked, chewed, sniffed, or used as a rather special seasoning in food for harmless but uniquely delightful results. 1 lid (1 oz.) $2.50; 6 lids (6 oz.) $10.00. Satisfaction guaranteed.

god is groovy, man

# 5. god is groovy, man

"CAN YOU DIG IT?"

"I KNOW YOU CAN DIG THAT ALMOST EVERYONE TODAY IS HUNG UP. WHY? BECAUSE YOU'VE BEEN SOLD A PHONEY BILL OF GOODS, NOT REALITY. YOU'VE LET THE CHURCHES PULL THE WOOL OVER YOUR EYES ABOUT JESUS, WHO HE REALLY IS.

I DON'T BLAME YOU FOR GETTING UP TIGHT WITH THE CHRISTIANITY MOST CHURCHES PEDDLE . . . THAT JESUS IS SOME KIND OF MIDDLE CLASS, MATERIALISTIC MILKTOAST CHARACTER WHO WANTS TO SPOIL YOUR BAG WITH A BUNCH OF RULES. HE'S NO NAMBY-PAMBY CAT! IN FACT, HE REALLY SOCKS IT TO YOU WITH SOME REALLY HEAVY STUFF.

HE TOOK THE RAP FOR YOU SO YOU COULD KNOW REAL LIFE. WE'VE BLOWN IT, BUT HE'S WILLING TO FORGET IT IF WE'LL JUST OWN UP THAT WE CAN'T GO IT ALONE AND ASK HIM TO HELP. HE MADE US SO HE'S GOT TO FIX US UP. ALL WE HAVE TO DO IS TAKE HIM FOR A FREE TICKET ON THAT ULTIMATE ETERNAL TRIP!

DO YOU WANT TO SHAKE YOUR HANG-UP? THEN JUST THANK HIM FOR TAKING THE RAP AND TAKE

HIM FOR YOUR BEST BUDDY.
CHECK IT OUT AND SEE IF THESE
THINGS HE SAID REALLY JIVE!
MAN, HE'S THE COOL ONE. BEING
ONE OF HIS HEP CATS IS BEING
WHERE IT'S AT.

HIS PROGRAM IS REALLY GROOVY
BUT IT'S TOUGH. IT DOESN'T
MEAN HAVING YOUR OWN BAG
AND DOING YOUR OWN THING:
YOU'VE GOT TO LOVE HIM MORE
THAN ANYTHING OR ANYBODY.
YOU'VE GOT TO DO GOD'S THING—
NOT YOUR OWN EGO TRIP. YOU'VE
GOT TO GO OUT OF YOUR WAY
AND HELP OTHER CATS SEE THE
LIGHT. IT MAY PUT YOU UP TIGHT
AND WRECK YOUR STATUS, BUT
HE'LL NEVER LET YOU DOWN.

SO, IF YOU CAN'T DIG THE SYSTEM,
GET HEP TO JESUS. READ THE
BIBLE, NOT WHAT SOME HANG-UP
NUT SAYS ABOUT IT. IF HE'S YOUR
BAG, IT'S A HEAVENLY TRIP. IF
NOT. BAD NEWS: YOU ARE ON AN
ETERNAL BUMMER. HE BUSTED
OUT FOR YOU. WHY NOT TUNE
IN TO HIM, TURN ON TO THE
BIBLE AND BUST OUT TO HIS
PEACE AND FREEDOM FOREVER."

"GOD IS GROOVY, MAN CAN YOU
DIG IT?"

So advertises David Berg, founder
and promoter of the hippie "Light Club" in Hunt-
ington Beach, Los Angeles, California. The purpose of this club, he says, is to help young people
find the way to Christ. He claims members of the
club are reformed hippies looking for truth. The
club is open daily until 2:00 A.M. and provides free
food, a place to relax, a prayer room and folk
entertainment. The songs, all with a religious mes-

sage, are sung by several followers of the group.
The long-haired, hippie-clothed audience sits silent
through the numbers, shouting "Amen" at the end
of each one. The minister has a "betrothal" ceremony in which former hippies and drug users are
"hooked up." He claims this Bible betrothal is akin
to engagement. After the ceremony, complete with
ring and a kiss, he gives a brief talk on how they
became members of the club.

The sandaled minister condemns the established
church as an institution and hopes for a revolt of
youth against it. "The greatest commandment today is don't miss church on Sunday. You can live
like hell the rest of the week as long as you enter
the church on Sunday. The church is about as far
away from what Christ preached as capitalism
and communism. All you guys that got busted are
in good company. Christ and all his followers were
put in jail, and so was I. You can't even stand, sit
or kneel on the sidewalks, if you've got long hair."
And with this Mr. Berg and his congregation head
for the beaches, singing and passing out free food,
hoping to create a spiritual revolution.

Berg is one of the new breed of ministers who
believes God is not dead—just that He's turned
"groovy." His brand of evangelism includes pop
songs, subtly interspersed with spiritual phrases.
Calling this type of evangelism "the new scene,"
hippie evangelists such as this one quote the Scrip-
tures with updated, mid-sixties hip dialect. They
invite their hippie friends to take the "ultimate
trip." Designed to be revolutionary, they preach
the gospel as a "hep" Christ, a "groovy" God, and
salvation as a "schtick."

I can tell you this is not the message nor the motif that will result in a lasting commitment to the Christian way. But what is the message that will get through to this runaway generation? First of all, the love message is definitely on the way out. As one young rebel put it, "The love scene is breaking up. We found that we could say almost anything in this country and people would not get upset. We could advocate destruction, bombing, corruption, murder, hate and all we'd get was a general put down. Then we tried the message of love but it was thrown right back in our faces. We tried 'finking out' but we just became ornaments to society. But now, brother, it's an eye for an eye and a tooth for a tooth. If bully cop comes on the scene, he better have his hand on his gun."

I believe this nation is on the brink of student unrest and rebellion the like of which we've never seen. Campuses are more like reservations and students now enjoy tribal togetherness. Like the Indians of the old West, they are hitting the warpath riding white horses of idealism. Tired of dreams, they want action now. They are prepared to fight the bloodiest battle in history in the name of peace.

Now, I'm a minister and not a politician. I want peace and I deplore war as much as any college rebel. I also know the price tag for freedom is often bloodshed.

I refuse to argue God's cause to this runaway generation. I will not defend the Gospel of the Lord Jesus Christ against those who have already hardened their hearts by way of an intellectual cop out. But I have some straight talk for high school and college students who have yet to find true freedom. The Bible is not silent concerning the rebel and the runaway. Let me give you God's message to students everywhere. It may not be "groovy" to you, but I assure you it is the truth that will set you free.

In the book of Judges there is the ancient, yet contemporary, story of a bearded, long-haired rebel, Samson, who wanted to overthrow the political system of his day:

Born into the family of a minority group, Samson spent his teenage years fretting about the corrupt, political establishment of the neighboring Philistines.

He was destined to greatness and was possessed with courage and inner strength. His cause was just and he was vitally interested in the human need around him. He had little time for the religious leaders who were playing with toy gods and idols. Samson shunned the materialistic world about him, even took a vow never to shave, or cut his hair.

This young rebel became obsessed with the desire to right civil injustices and to wipe out the poverty of his people. There was a new message in the wind and Samson could hear it. He was not a peaceful demonstrator by any stretch of the imagination. He became an activist. This rebel looted thirty changes of clothing and killed thirty men in the process. He caught three hundred foxes and tied fire-brands to their tails and set them running through the corn fields of the rival political party. He burned their corn, their vineyards and their olive orchards. This violence started a riot in the establishment. In retaliation they burned the houses of his own poverty-stricken people. In revenge, Samson, who had become the strongest man in the world, removed the huge gates of the city of Gaza and carried them into the mountains.

Samson's own people decried his demonstrations and demanded law and order. Weary of violence, they delivered him to the Philistines. Just when it appeared that Samson had lost his cause, the spirit of the Lord came upon him, he broke loose, picked up the jawbone of an ass and killed one thousand Philistine national guardsmen.

At this point the story becomes even more relevant for this young rebel developed a steak of childishness. He began sitting on the grass, wasting time with flower children and tossing around riddles. From there his next step down was the bed of a harlot and final doom.

Samson is a prototype of this runaway generation. Samson, the one man who could have made the difference, who could have overthrown the establishment, ended his life in one big bloody act of violence.

Now let me sock it to you. Your beards and your long hair don't bother me. Wearing kooky clothes won't send you to hell. You tell me that you are interested in human need, civil injustice, and that you want to wipe out poverty. You tell me the church is dead and the political system is corrupt and the establishment is a rat race. You tell me you are angry because so many people are prejudiced and that you want to help wipe out all discrimination. Good for you!

I don't mind your waving banners and carrying flags or demonstrating because of your social concern and because you want to be involved. Even though it hurts me to say it, I must also agree with you that parents can be phoney and that this is an age of dishonesty. But, if you are so concerned and your cause is so just, what in the world are you doing sitting around in the grass hung up on some foolish habit and tossing around riddles?

Like Samson, many young intellectual fools are trading courage for childishness. They are losing their voice, their power and their influence because they are strung out with sensuous hang-ups, preaching idealism, truth and honesty while laying around with prostitutes, preaching peace while blowing pot, incurring the wrath of society through stupid acts of violence.

The revolution is on! Young, modern Samsons refuse to heed the lessons of history. The roof is ready to cave in. These young runaways are ready to die and they don't mind taking others with them.

My message to the young intellectual is,

Don't
be a
fool
for a
fool
cause
and
die a
fool's
death.

Don't
mistake
childishness
for
courage.

Don't
mistake
weirdness
for
wisdom.

Don't
mistake
lewdness
for
love.

Don't
mistake
violence
for
victory.

GET
smart
and
get
your
education.

LOOK
for the
right
things
in the
right
places.

LEARN
all
about
what
Jesus
said
and
did.

SEEK
truth
in
God's Word.

His
Holy Spirit
will
guide
to

peace—
purpose.

The Bible says, "It is better to hear the rebuke of the wise than for a man to hear the song of fools" (Ecclesiastes 7:5).

To all my minister friends around the world who want to reach the runaway generation, let me add this. You cannot win rebels by being like them. Put away your childish talk. God is not "groovy" or "hep" and Christ is not a "cool cat." Jargon does not make the Gospel relevant; it is still the simple preaching of the cross of Jesus Christ that leads to redemption. Take off your love beads and grow up! If you become a mixer, you're going to get mixed up. You're not going to reach this generation by what you say—but by what you are and by the way you live.

To church leaders, I say the church is not a cheap crash pad for hippies. God's house is not a theatre for hippie happenings. It is the staging area for sinners who would be rocketed to spiritual heights of wonder and reality through faith in Jesus Christ, the Way, the Truth and the Life.

God is not groovy, man—God is great!

the wagumps

# 6. the wagumps

> "The world is like a board with holes
> in it, and the square men have got
> into the round holes, and the round
> into the square."
>
> Bishop Berkeley

There were thirty of them creating a most unusual scene. While the flags of many nations waved in the breeze, on the street below thirty young people, all wrapped contiguously in a mammoth white sheet, paraded back and forth in front of the United Nations building. These were not bearded, unkempt youth—they were clean! The boys had shaved their beards, some had shaven heads; bald pates glistened in the noonday sun. Who were they? The wagumps!

The wagumps assert that the hippies are dead. The yippies are almost dead. And they are the movement which will replace them both. The wagumps prevail in Manhattan's lower east side, in a small colony in suburban Mt. Kisco, New York, in Los Angeles, and San Francisco. They are spreading to other cities throughout the United States and around the world. More than eight thousand people subscribe to their bi-weekly newsletter which consists of two blank pages of white paper.

They dress in white and strut along the streets as

paragons of cleanliness. Wagump couples soap each other in a ceremony called a "washout." Theatrical events called "Nothings" are presented in dark halls and alleys—nothing.

The wagump movement is secretive and mysterious having no recognized name and wanting none. Its followers simply call it, "the movement." The word wagump does not mean anything in any language and is merely used to describe individual members.

In an effort to break away from conventional language, wagumps refer to each other as "you" or "thou" and then tab a number to it. "You 77" refers to a baldheaded youth of about nineteen who lives in an empty room entirely covered with felt and green and blue rugs. "We are trying," he said, "to cut ourselves free from the umbilical cord of society. We don't want to be called hippies or yippies and resent old words. We want to be free to wallow in our own peaches and cream."

Wagumps say they are involved in "sensory perception." Influenced by the Hindus, the wagumps preach a message of total cleanliness and promulgate the idea that sin and impurity can be washed away physically. By wearing white and engaging in ceremonial washings, the wagumps seek to provide a supportive environment that simulates the purity of mind they hope to achieve. While the hippies talked about "loving," the wagumps talk about "feeling." The wagumps have no slogans. Their posters have nothing words, with nothing messages such as "Railroads Through Eternity," or "Trigonometry Drinks Cocoa."

Wagumps claim to have learned a lesson from

the failure of hippie life. They argue that, if you drop out of society completely, you just recreate its corruptions on a different level. Whereas the hippies are afraid to establish meaningful relationships, the wagumps feel their contacts should be selective, sincere, and even more meaningful. They place more emphasis on impulses than actions.

They scoff at the idea of involvement and violent revolution. They claim to be in a revolution of touch, movement and the joy of feeling. They have nothing to do with the theatre, music, painting, sculpture. Even literature is a waste of time and effort. Their thing is "live-in feeling."

The wagumps have resolved to do away with any experience that is too demanding of the mind. They delight in sitting cross-legged in their felt-lined rooms, rubbing hands over the pile and receiving a blessing. Perhaps more honest than the phoney art critics of this generation, they denounce modern art as "tedious dirt." Art objects are called "feelies." Art, they claim, lies in the texture of its surface and in the weight and balance of the object.

Wagumps don't like to talk about sex. However, "You 22" confessed, "We make love like a bunch of celery—with a single stalk. We practice the old Indo-Chinese method of orgasm by implosion."

"Wash outs" or "group baths" bring the community closer together. By washing one another they claim to wash away tensions. Their homes are decorated with a bottle of Kleen. A box of Oxydol— "The Wash Day Miracle"—is a symbol of the movement. Wagumps wear white as a symbol of cleanliness and purity. It is seen as a sign of the absence of vice and every act of cleanliness is another attempt to wash away hang-ups.

Is this all a put-up? Not on your Lifebuoy! Though the wagumps are relatively few in number, their potential influence is great and their message is spreading. They claim to be passing through a state of "nothingness" preparing for a super-Christ who is soon to be revealed to the world.

This movement is most symbolic, for the coming of two Christs is indeed predicted in the Bible—Christ, The Son of the Living God, and the antichrist.

So, today while the children of the Living God prepare themselves with the white robes of true righteousness which are given by faith, the children of the antichrist wash themselves with soap and water and wrap themselves in robes of self-righteousness.

This would indicate the present generation of runaways is tired of the sin, the emptiness, the foolishness and the futility of the hippie way of life. Now the runaways are going from one extreme to the other. From beards to no beards, from long hair to no hair, from ear piercing psychedelic sounds to quiet contemplation and feeling—a baby blanket or a rug. Formerly they did not bathe for months on end; they now bathe every hour on the hour. They have rebelled against the phoney art and empty literature of the psychedelic revolution and now embrace the empty world of nothingness.

I believe it was inevitable that the wagumps should appear on the American scene. They are an important symbol that screams a message of urgency to the church. That urgent message is simply this: The young want to be clean. They want someone to show them the way to holiness, purity and purpose. They need more than the cleansing power of Oxydol—they need the ultrabrightness of Christ, the Light of the World.

sex in the seaweed

# 7. sex in the seaweed

> "Virtue is an angel, but she is a blind one, and must ask of knowledge to show her the pathway that leads to her goal."
>
> Horace Mann

A little known "sex juice" drug is being circulated among teenagers at New Jersey shore resorts; it induces wilder, but shorter trips than LSD and can be bought by mail. The drug is known as "sex juice" or as "68." Distributed in sugar cubes, it has not been exhaustively analyzed, but one toxicologist compares the substance to other hallucinatory drugs such as LSD.

The drug may also be purchased by mail in the form of a blotter soaked in "68." There are one hundred micrograms of the drug per square inch; the user simply snips off a portion of the blotter and sucks it. A "68" trip lasts three to four hours, as compared to an LSD trip which lasts from eight to twelve hours. Users claim that just a few minutes after taking a cube of "68" they experience a violent, epileptic-type seizure and that something suddenly explodes in the brain. Although experts have warned the drug may be extremely dangerous, its use is spreading.

"Sex in the seaweed" suggests that the meaning

73

and purpose of sex is being lost in a sea of hallucinations induced by weeds such as marijuana and other narcotics. Sex to the cop out crowd is ugly, difficult and empty—not the beautiful experience God intended it to be.

Statistics indicate three thousand new cases of venereal disease are reported every day in the United States and more than one million illegal abortions are performed annually. Three hundred thousand illegitimate births are recorded each year though fourteen states keep no record of legitimacy. There is an alarming increase in illicit sexual activity. Pregnancy is the most frequent physical condition for which girls now leave school.

It is estimated that one out of sixteen girls will become pregnant out of wedlock before she reaches twenty. These unwanted pregnancies occur not only to backward mountain girls or prostitutes, but also to single girls from every social and economic background.

Why this sudden and alarming rise in v.d.?

Why are so many teenagers having illegitimate babies?

The answer to these questions is, in part, the answer to why so many kids are running away from home. Rejection by parents is one of the main reasons I've been given by girls who were pregnant before running away. And the reason given by many girls for getting pregnant was that they felt unloved at home and were seeking affection.

A fifteen-year-old girl from Los Angeles listened as I counseled young people to be respectful and loving to their parents. She later stopped me in the lobby of the auditorium and begged me to listen to her story.

She said, "It's all right for you to tell teenagers how to act toward parents, but I think parents should be told to be more loving toward us. My dad is a successful businessman and a deacon in the church. I'm not really a bad girl, but as you can see, I'm pregnant. When my mother came home from the doctor and told Dad about it, he blew up. He called me a dirty tramp and told me I'd have to leave the house or I'd ruin his business. They put me in a foster home and that's where I am now. I think parents should stick with their kids no matter what happens. I need my parents now, more than I've ever needed them in my life."

There are more than one hundred and sixty-five private shelters and maternity homes for unwed mothers in America. Yet, many expectant unwed mothers never reach them. Too often, they pack up a few belongings and head for Haight Ashbury or Greenwich Village, believing they will be accepted.

Scientists intended "the pill" to be used by married couples to prevent unwanted pregnancies. However, it has had a morally devastating impact upon numerous unmarried girls. Misguided mothers give their daughters "the pill," rather than teaching them morality.

One of the greatest arguments against sex before marriage has been the fear of pregnancy. Now, "the pill" is here and it is possible for girls to be free from this fear. But this does not free them from responsibility. If the use of "the pill" results in making the sex act just a release or a diversion, it becomes a curse to society. This is the reason sex for the runaway generation is becoming tiresome and often disgusting. Many young prostitutes have come to us seeking help. More than once I've heard them say, "It's a dog's life."

Unless sex is guided by the true values of life, founded upon a marriage deeply rooted in genuine love, it becomes animalistic and the total effect is extremely harmful to the person. I personally believe the use of pills, among the unmarried, causes an improper balance between the physical, mental and spiritual being. It creates an overemphasis on only one aspect of human experience. I believe "the pill" is often used as a cop out by mothers and fathers who don't want to exercise their responsibility toward their children. They don't take the time to ask where their daughters are going or with whom. Many parents are too busy with their own lives, jobs, running to parties and clubs.

Sex in the seaweed is also fostered by prevailing attitudes toward censorship. A Congressional Committee estimated seventy-five per cent of all obscene material fell into the hands of young people and that the amount of money spent on pornography exceeded a half billion dollars annually.

Pornography in its varied media has caused a tragic moral landslide. Pre-teens are constantly exposed to sex, violence and sadism in "adult type" motion pictures. They are bombarded by scenes of zombies, vampires and monsters—the screen bathed in blood and decapitations. On any Saturday afternoon they can see such hideous stuff as "Jack the

Ripper," in bloody vision. Films that have been banned in Europe are seen by American children. Such motion pictures have definitely fostered the development of the "seaweed sex" situation.

There is no question that pornography implants in the young an unhealthy preoccupation with sex. The endless diet of pornography has had the effect of awakening sexual appetites without providing an understanding of moral values. Indeed, it is difficult to match the parents' teaching against the full-color dramatic obscenities being pushed by the smut peddlers.

Don't try to tell me to get off my soapbox. And don't give me any more lip about censorship and freedom of the press. I am fed up with people who call obscene movies, "art films." Of course, I don't believe we can legislate holiness to our teenagers. Cleaning up bookstands won't clean up the minds of youth. We must effectively teach high moral standards and mold the characters of our young people so they will have the inner strength to withstand the pressures of smut and pornography. Coupled with this, the avalanche of dirt has to be stopped.

It seems to me we need chastity courses in the curricula of our schools and colleges. Our young people need to be taught that sex must be equated with responsibility, and that freedom requires character, strength of purpose and the courage to say no. Furthermore, they should be taught that all sex outside of marriage is sinful. Thousands of hippies have lost themselves in sex in the seaweed, but it is never to late to wake up and face a new beginning. King David once stood before the casket of his dead, illegitimate child holding hands with the wife he stole. But David was forgiven, he acknowledged his sin to God and turned away from it. David said, "this poor man cried and the Lord heard him and delivered him out of all his troubles."

Thank God there are still millions of young people who choose to live clean, moral lives. There are still enough kids in this nation without sexual hangups that I feel like shouting, "hallelujah!"

the "jim chromies"

# 8. the "jim chromies"

> "After all there is but one race—humanity."
>
> George Moore

Thousands of white young people have "Negrophobia." The symptoms include guilt attitudes regarding the treatment of black people, resentment of the racist attitude held by the older generation and an obsession to expedite the process of equality and justice. While some are on the level and accomplish meaningful goals, others have merely camouflaged their "Jim Crow" beliefs.

Jim Crow is the practice of segregation as applied to Negroes in the United States. Although Jim Crow laws which compelled segregation have been abolished, the attitude persists. But in an effort to whitewash Jim Crowism, people have developed what I call, "Jim Chromeism"—or black icing. It is window dressing, tokenism and decorative acts of phoney love and equality. Much of which parades under the banner of brotherhood, justice and equal rights is nothing but chrome. It is a shining, insincere cover-up for the unbending posture of Jim Crowism.

A "Jim Chromie" goes to Alabama to demonstrate and sing, "We Shall Overcome," but then returns to his pretty suburb to attend a community meeting called to keep a Negro family from moving into the area.

A "chromie" pastor in the guise of integration, searches for a "good nigger," preferably a professional who lives in a good home and has a good reputation, so that he can invite him to become a member, then goes to his ministerial meeting and boasts of his integrated church.

A "chromie" white girl dates a black boy just to prove that she is above prejudice or to spite her parents.

A "chromie" politician pushes integration and then enrolls his own kids in a private school.

A "chromie" suburbanite goes into a Negro ghetto once a year, equipped with a bucket of paint, a brush and a ladder and covers the filth and the curse words on dilapidated buildings and then lectures to his neighbors about involvement and compassion.

A "chromie" individual tries to cure his Negrophobia by donating $50.00 to the Martin Luther King Memorial Fund.

A "chromie" Negro spews vitriolic curses at "whitey" and then dates white girls.

A "Jim Chromie" ministerial association imports two or three black families into its neighborhood just to scratch their itch of involvement.

"Chromeism" is the process whereby employers hire blacks to meet a certain percentage quota in order to keep government contracts, or, place the prettiest black girls in the front office to give the impression that they are not prejudiced.

"Chromeism" is a procedure whereby colleges

permit a few outstanding black students to enroll in an effort to avoid a confrontation with the militants.

A study by Glock-Stark revealed that 50 per cent of the Catholics and Protestants in California said they would seek housing elsewhere if a black family moved in next door. Seventy per cent of those interviewed denounced clergy involvement in civil rights. The report concluded, "The majority of laity continues to bare ill will toward other races and religions. They may claim to love their brothers, but are finicky about whom they call 'brother.'"

Young people today are justly critical of parents who attend church and piously sing, "Blest Be the Tie That Binds Our Hearts in Christian Love" and then refuse a Negro's entrance into the church. They are growing impatient and ask, "If God exists, why doesn't He do something about this? Is the adult generation too deeply involved in tradition and deep-seated racial fears to change?" I feel there has to be a change, but it must be the result of genuine love not just chrome.

I have conducted outdoor youth crusades in stadiums of major cities in South Africa. One of the white evangelical ministers in Johannesburg shocked me by earnestly stating, "The black man has no soul." I cannot begin to describe the hurt I felt as I arrived at the stadium in that great city and found the blacks seated outside. When I made an effort to open the stands and invite the blacks to be seated in the main sections, I was told that if I did, a great many "Christians" would walk out and I might even be asked to leave the country.

Perhaps the most difficult moment came for me when I invited young people to the altar to surrender their lives to Christ. According to the rules, when the invitation was extended, the whites approached from one side and the blacks from the other. I stood on that platform and observed a sea of young black faces to my left and a sea of young white faces to my right—and I was shattered! I whispered a prayer, "Oh God, no wonder so many of these kids have given up on the church and Christianity. They have been taught they are not equal, that You have set a wall between them and it must not be penetrated. Help me to break it down."

Those who stood before me were well-dressed, intelligent South Africans of both races. For the next two hours, I mingled with them, prayed for them, and listened as they unburdened their hearts to me. At first the Negro teenagers were afraid to shake my hand. They seemed to cower at the sight of a white man walking through "enemy" territory. But before long they put their arms around me and sobbed as they reached out to God from the depths of their hearts. I found them to be the warmest and friendliest people I've met anywhere in the world. But even more encouraging was the attitude present among the young people that night. They gave me the impression, that with half a chance, they would overthrow the apartheid situation. I am quick to add that in spite of the racial prejudice of so many in South Africa, I found a number of saintly people who had as much true love for Negroes as anyone in the world.

The South African government has grand displays of Jim Chromeism. Visitors are taken on a tour through the many sprawling building projects for blacks and are shown staggering figures of the cost of welfare projects. As world pressure mounts against apartheid, in my opinion, still more chromeism will appear.

Tension spawned by prejudice is prevalent almost everywhere. In the United States there is tension between Negroes and whites and in Canada between French and English. A volcano of prejudice has erupted in Ireland, Spain and South America between Catholics and Protestants. In Central and Northern Africa, I witnessed tribal prejudice beyond description. The whole world is guilty! But what can one young person do about it? Would he be wasting motion as if he were emptying the ocean with a bucket? No, God has always used individuals to change the world. God's call has always been "Who will go? Who will rise up against evil-doers?"

David, a teenage shepherd, heard the giant, Goliath, mock his entire nation. Everyone, including his older brothers, was paralyzed by fear. But this young man heard God's call. He was convinced there was no giant too big for his God to conquer. God needed a volunteer and David was ready to lay his life on the line.

David made the difference. What about you? Where do you stand? As one individual you can rid your heart of bitterness and prejudice. You can refrain from telling or listening to racial jokes. If you are Negro, you can stop calling white people "whitey" or "honkey." Everyone can eliminate "nigger," "spic," "dago" and all other racial nicknames. You can work hard at being a good example of love and understanding. You can treat all minority groups with dignity and respect. You can quit judging people by the way they dress or where they live. You can speak out against discrimination, strife, hatred and misunderstanding everywhere you see it. You can learn to practice what you preach.

Most important of all, you can forget chromeism and root out prejudice which is self love. God, who once wrote His laws in stone, now writes His laws with love in the hearts of men. This generation which talks so glibly about love refuses to recognize that God is the source of it. Love can not be legislated. What legislation has failed to do, God wants and is willing to do by His power working through those who are available.

If people had love they would not be tormented by fear, because the Bible says, "There is no fear in love, but perfect love casts out fear ... he who fears is not perfected in love" (I John 4:18 RSV).

God's Word continues with this statement which is stronger than any I have heard from racial activists on the American scene.

"If any one says, 'I love God,' and hates his brother, *he is a liar;* for he who does not love his brother whom he has seen, cannot love God whom he has not seen. And this commandment we have from him, that he who loves God should love his brother also" (I John 4:20, 21 rsv).

God's love in the hearts of men will outshine chromeism.

the "shims"

# 9. the "shims"

> "Style is the dress of thoughts."
> Chesterfield

A Riddle:

What has two feet, long hair, a Peter Pan collar, pearl buttons, a gorgeous necklace, perfectly manicured nails, alligator purse, pastel britches, zipper boots, and walks like a princess?

It's a she.

Take a closer look.

It's a *him!*

Another Riddle:

What has two feet, short hair, a black leather jacket, levi pants, hush puppy shoes, a masculine straw hat, smells of perspiration and swaggers like a wrestler?

It's a him.

Take a closer look.

It's a *she!*

But who knows?

We could both be wrong.

It could be a "shim."

If you can't tell whether it is a "she" or a "him," it has to be a "shim."

It is becoming more and more difficult to distinguish between the sexes. It's Halloween almost every night in Haight Ashbury, Greenwich Village,

and Yorkville in Toronto. If this ludicrous trend
toward sartorial camouflage were not so tragic, it
would be comical.

> Some appear to be:
> Cowboys
> Indians
> Daniel Boone
> Tribal chiefs
> Prophets
> Bonnie
> and
> Clyde
> wearing
> bells
> beads
> feathers
> prayer chains
> incense pots
> saris
> hoods
> capes
> veils
> trinkets
> bracelets
> love symbols
> nose rings
> earrings
> ornamental buttons
> army fatigues
> bell bottom trousers
> boots
> moccasins

This assortment of personalized styles is designed to give individual identity.

I saw a young man walking down a street of Haight Ashbury with a white rat on his shoulder with a gold chain hanging around its neck. Asked why he paraded around with a white rat with a gold chain, he answered, "Do you see anyone else with a white rat and a gold chain? This makes me different."

Today's confusion of styles is only a symptom of the tumultuous condition of the inner man. It is a fact of history that in every moral landslide preceding the judgement of God on a generation, men have adopted an unusual manner of dress. In the motion picture production, "The Bible," the producers clothed all Noah's mockers in hippie-type apparel just prior to the flood. In the same movie, the Sodomites, who came to harass Lot and his visitors, were dressed in various costumes much like those worn by hippies today.

The prophet Isaiah lived in a day of moral erosion similar to ours. In the third chapter of his prophecy he said, ". . . youth will be insolent to the elder, and the base fellow to the honorable" (Isaiah 3:5 RSV). He spoke of homosexuals and Sodomites who refused to "hide their sins." It was a day of oppression, error and destruction. There was violence on every side. He told of a great war coming and many men being killed. In that crucial hour, just before the downfall, Isaiah took his generation to task for their weird dress and daring ornamentation:

"The Lord said: Because the daughters of Zion

are haughty and walk with outstretched necks, glancing wantonly with their eyes, mincing along as they go, tinkling with their feet; the Lord will smite with a scab the heads of the daughters of Zion, and the Lord will lay bare their secret parts. In that day the Lord will take away the finery of the anklets, the headbands, and the crescents; the pendants, the bracelets, and the scarfs; the headdresses, the armlets, the sashes, the perfume boxes, and the amulets, the signet rings, and nose rings; the festal robes, the mantles, the cloaks, and the handbags; the garments of gauze, the linen garments, the turbans, and the veils."

(Isaiah 3: 16-23)

Some of today's fashions are being styled by homosexual designers. Fashions that were once worn only in the underground as "drag" are now being sold in the best houses in the land. I believe there is a definite attempt being made by the homosexual community to "effeminize" the young generation.

A recent issue of a national homosexual magazine advocates a "homosexual revolution." It pointed to the relaxed religious and political attitudes toward homosexuality. The signs of this relaxed trend are evidenced by advertisements, similar to this one, which appear regularly in various newspapers.

HOW TO MEET MR. RIGHT

YOU CAN NOW MEET THE REALLY RIGHT PEOPLE THE SAFE, DIGNIFIED,

CONFIDENTIAL WAY. IT USED TO BE DIFFICULT TO MEET PEOPLE WHO SHARE YOUR INTERESTS, PEOPLE WITH THAT JUST RIGHT PERSONALITY, LOOKS, TASTES AND BACKGROUND. SPACE AGE COMPUTER SCIENCE NOW MAKES IT SAFER AND EASIER FOR YOU TO MAKE THE FRIEND YOU'VE ALWAYS WANTED TO MAKE . . . THE TRULY DISCREET WAY.

GAY POWER HAS NOW MADE AVAILABLE AN I.B.M. 360 COMPUTER DATING SERVICE SPECIALLY DESIGNED BY GAY PEOPLE FOR THE EXCLUSIVE USE OF THE HOMOSEXUAL COMMUNITY.

WHATEVER YOUR PRACTICAL INTERESTS, OUR COMPUTER CAN NOW FIND SOMEONE TO MATCH YOUR DESIRES. YOU ARE SURE TO MEET AT LEAST 5 AND UP TO 14 COMPATIBLE PEOPLE.

NO MATTER WHERE YOU LIVE IN THE USA, THE COMPUTER WILL WORK TO FIND MATCHES FOR YOU RIGHT IN YOUR VERY OWN AREA.

CALL OR WRITE TODAY FOR FREE ILLUSTRATED LITERATURE.

Homosexual organizations are springing up all over the country with the purpose of "dedicating themselves to respond to the needs and desires of homosexuals everywhere." Some of the homosexual organizations now seeking acceptance for their kind are: Mattachine Society, Janus Society, Phoenix Society, Association for Social Knowledge, Association for Responsible Citizenship, Daughters of Bilitis, Tangents, Council on Religion and the Homophile, Pride, One, Inc., The Council on Religion and the Homosexual, The Tavern Guild, Citizens News, and SIR (Society for Individual Rights).

Police in San Francisco have estimated that eighty to ninety thousand San Franciscans, or more than ten per cent of the city's seven hundred and ninety-thousand people, are homosexuals. One of the greatest allies or protectors for the homosexual community in San Francisco is the "Glide Foundation" of Glide Memorial Methodist Church. Glide Memorial was built in 1930 as an evangelistic center. Today, the church holds "soul gigs" (rock and roll concerts) in its sanctuary. It sponsors retreats for clergymen and homosexuals and dances for male prostitutes.

I have personally observed the Glide Foundation in operation and am convinced that some of its ministers are dedicated and well meaning but the homosexual community has taken advantage of the church.

One national underground magazine written especially for the gay set, warns that society may soon try to legislate against "long hair, earrings, boots and allied adornments." The warning was directed especially to hippie homosexuals who live in the Tenderloin area of downtown San Francisco.

Must we legislate against long hair, weird clothes and the sexual aberrations they often represent? Shall we condemn the shims and tell them that they are hopelessly bound and headed for hell without a chance of recovery? Shall we try to capture all the runaways, cut off their beards, and throw them into a bath?

Let me lay it on the line! I cannot accept the Glide approach of running babysitting services for homosexuals. I believe that Christ can cure the homosexual who really wants help. Paul the Apostle makes it clear that certain homosexuals in Corinth were delivered from this bondage. Nothing is impossible with God and I'll stake my life and ministry on that!

I'm not putting down boys with long hair, but let me tell you what the Bible says:

"Does not even nature itself teach you that, for a man to wear long hair is degrading to him?" ( I Corinthians 11:14)

I can understand why a hippie wears effeminate or weird clothes; it is all a part of a confusion pattern. But I cannot accept the weird dress, the beards and the love beads worn by so many workers who are trying to help hippies. I have met ministers dressed as shims, who wore long hair, beards, and hippie clothes so they would be accepted. I have worked with drug addicts for eleven years and I never had to dress like one to win one. The addicts go unshaven, don't change clothes for weeks; don't comb their hair and seldom bathe.

Must I show them my love by adopting their habits? Never!

Some of the new fashions today are chic and most attractive. Many of these fashions can be worn by Christian young people without any sense of guilt or self condemnation. But after working with thousands of runaway kids all over the world, I can testify that the first step toward the hippie life frequently is the desire to wear off-beat clothes. Young people who are truly satisfied with Jesus Christ and who have a deep inner peace do not need the attention or the kicks that come from looking outlandish.

If the only thing that can make you stand out in a crowd is a white rat with a gold chain, better go get one. If the only personal identification you can find is in looking like an escapee from the zoo, get into the costume parade and be a fruitnik. But if you really want to stand out in the crowd—if you want true identity—then be really different. Let your mark of individuality be characterized by "... love, joy, peace, patience, kindness, goodness, faithfulness, gentleness, self-control" (Galatians 5:22).

the "junkies"

# 10. the "junkies"

"I tell you the past is a bucket of ashes."
Carl Sandburg (Prairie)

GIRL, THIRTEEN, TAKES LSD TRIP IN SCHOOL

This was the headline in a recent New York City newspaper. The article stated in part:

"Intensive investigation is underway into the use of drugs in a Bronx Junior High School, following the startling discovery of a thirteen-year-old girl writhing in 'another world' on the floor of a lavatory under the influence of LSD. A fourteen-year-old girl was also removed from class for erratic behavior. She was found 'screaming and crawling on her stomach,' in a state of malfunction. On the previous Friday, three girls were taken from the school in obvious states of stupor.

It was also revealed that four other students, ranging in age from twelve to fourteen, had been hospitalized, all apparently under the influence of narcotics.

Special teams have been assigned to find the

source of the narcotics. Parents and teachers are cooperating."

A discussion among seniors at a large Catholic boy's high school on Long Island revealed that only 6 boys in the class had not tried drugs. In a prosperous Westchester community a school principal admitted that more than 30 per cent of the students were using narcotics on a regular basis and that more than 10 per cent had already become hardcore users.

"Junkies" (hardcore narcotics users) are one of the most tragic by-products of the runaway generation. Marijuana (grass) almost without exception was an important step along the drug route.

There are nearly seventeen million public high school students in America, and as many as two million of them are smoking marijuana, or using other narcotics. Marijuana, like the other hallucinogens, can sometimes produce a state of paranoia (feelings of persecution) and this is the beginning of what I call the "route." Some teenagers become hostile, aggressive, extroverted and possibly homicidal, while others become weak, fearful and uncertain; others attempt suicide.

A nickel bag of pot ($5.00) makes twelve joints (cigarettes). That's just about 41¢ each. LSD costs anywhere from $5.00 to $20.00 depending on the length of the trip desired. Marijuana is the easiest narcotic to obtain. It is also easy to grow.

A high school teacher in Los Angeles was arrested for growing marijuana plants in windowboxes. He sold it to students to "hallucinate and illuminate their minds."

A Long Island father brought his hippie son to me for counseling. The boy had no motivation or interest in work. After a few weeks, the father called to say that his son had become interested in agriculture for, "He is always in the backyard digging in the ground." Later we were shocked to learn the police had destroyed the boy's garden; he had been growing marijuana!

In New Jersey, bird watchers reported seeing pigeons fluttering erratically. Investigation uncovered the startling fact that they were drugged after feeding on marijuana plants hidden among the foxtails and sunflowers in the Hackensack River meadowlands. It was learned the producers of birdseed had added marijuana to their product which made the canaries sing better. Housewives discarded the bird's droppings in the garbage, which was eventually dumped in the meadowlands. Some of the marijuana seeds germinated, explaining the growth of the plant in the area.

The marijuana was so thick that a truck load could be gathered rather quickly, an armful reaped in a few minutes. An average plant produces a half pound of marijuana. It was estimated twenty thousand plants were growing in the meadows, over ten thousand pounds of the stuff—enough to provide a joint for each of the seventeen million high school students in the country!

As founder of TEEN CHALLENGE, New York City, I have worked with as many narcotic addicts as any other man in the world. I have buried those who have died of an overdose or who have been murdered by pushers. I have gone to help young runaways who "tripped out" on LSD and other synthetics. And, although I have covered the narcotic problem in two of my previous books, I must say something here about the horrors of addiction and where it all ends.

Let me take you away from flashing lights and psychedelic sounds, away from the giddiness of a pot party and away from the subtle suggestions you see in movies that marijuana is "groovy." Let me show you the wages this sin inevitably pays.

I receive thousands of letters from teenagers all over the world. Recently a letter came from a young college student who was near death. Her letter is so tragic, so true, that I asked her permission to share it with you.

"Dear Mr. Wilkerson:
As far as is known, I am the only person who has injected cyanide and lived more than five minutes. I am still somewhat alive after two years.

I got the cyanide in an advanced narcotic called mescaline. If I had known that night what I knew the next morning, I would gladly have died of strangulation. I somehow struggled through the convulsions, each time sure that I was in the last and would get better. The hospitals here are not equipped to deal with such patients; so I was sent to Upstate Medical Center.

Most basic to the problem is the destruction of brain cells. The part of the medulla which controls the breathing function is eaten away completely. When I had surgery last November it was discovered that, as everyone else, I inhale by vacuum in the lungs, but that the air is forced out again by fluid in the plural cavity around the lungs. They tried to drain the fluid and discovered that it was blood from an unknown but unimportant source which was being released into the cavity at just the right pressure to carry on the breathing function. Unfortunately though, the right lung is now completely collapsed and the left one has to be drained frequently. The cyanide damaged my heart and the two times when my breathing has stopped, the heart has been severely damaged due to a lack of oxygen. There is kidney and liver damage and the only way to predict what may still occur is by referring to autopsy reports from two other victims.

By far the most hideous effect has been the change in physical appearance because of a mysterious change in the bone marrow which most of the time prevents it from producing red blood cells. Previously I was given several pints of blood a week. Now I have had none for almost three weeks. But the effect of this is much the same as the effect of Hodgkins Disease, bloating, etc. I weigh less than 150 pounds normally, but can bloat to 225/230 pounds within a few days. All of those things interact destructively. In order to breathe, I have oxygen available all the time. I am limited in the use of my arms because of the heart and lungs, yet because of an old back injury I must use crutches part of the time.

Extensive surgical repair of my lung could be attempted but I would never make it. Yet without surgery it is merely a time game. All of these things happen apparently to anyone ingesting cyanide but all other known victims have simply convulsed, strangled and died within three to five minutes. Even the effort expended cannot prevent my death, but the fact that death has been stalled off this long makes me a medical oddity.

I have gone through three procedures and have taken experimental medication like you would not believe. I complained but to no avail. They could care less; but being a guinea pig entails being an object for teaching. I drank radioactive B12 every morning and when one horrified doctor objected to the inhumanity of it, I hear someone say, 'You can't destroy a vegetable.' And today *I am a vegetable*, dependent on oxygen and respirators, blood and drugs. And most of all, anyone who wants to come by and, for a fleeting moment hold my hand, that I might know a strengthening to go on.

About my work, hobbies, etc., my basic thing is education. I had done my undergraduate work at Harpur and was enrolled in graduate courses split between Cortland and Scranton University when this happened.

I was hospitalized from the spring of 1966 until the following November. I was optimistic when released but went into the screaming meamies, practically, when I was told two weeks later that I must go back. I ran like 'hell' thinking that I could leave death behind. January 10, I believe it was, I went back, this time to the top floor of the hospital where patients are kept separate because their appearances are so altered by disease or injury. They have one more thing in common; they will never leave that place. It was horrible, because such patients cease to be people and become objects. It isn't meant to be this way, but a staff member cannot have any satisfaction when all his patients die, so he stops caring. Patients become either very intense or very aloof. There are almost no visitors ... friends and even families steel themselves to forget and these people are reckoned already dead. A funeral is but a formality.

Since the hospital opened in 1964 or 1965 only one patient before me was released from the eighth floor. When I was released, that was a big day for me; I had been there from January 10 until last summer and then was allowed to walk out. My fear of the eighth floor bordered on paranoia; under no circumstances will I ever return to Upstate. I made the decision to leave, being told that with the equipment there I could possibly live until another complication set in; but that in leaving I would have separated myself from their respiration facilities and would not have enough strength if I stopped breathing, to get to a hospital. It is not living in a place like that so I left.

One doctor from New York wanted to operate on my lungs. I stayed out for the rest of the summer then went into Loundes Hospital last October 23. That was pretty bad. I was not released until last month.

In October I was given four months to live. Somehow I am doing better than is medically expected. I had to go back for a few days the first of this month for blood and lung drainage. But now I have an apartment and am taking two courses at Harpur. My doctor finally understood that for my mental well being, I had to do something I felt was worthwhile. I am so close to my degree and I have secret aims of finishing it. I can keep going only if I sleep most of the time with an oxygen mask. I have oxygen tanks in the apartment now and do not go out much because I just do not have the stamina. After lung drainage, I felt that I did not need the oxygen because I could breathe so much better. I didn't use it and consequently went into a coma for four days. The police found me. I have been in much longer comas and they are always frightening.

So, you see, I haven't had much time to work or much strength to carry on hobbies. I'm afraid. I am on welfare now and I hate it, but I can do little about it. I started tutoring but had to give it up. It was fun because I had taught school for three years and I enjoy teenagers. Most of all, I just want to be occupied with something worthwhile.

It would be so good to talk with you again; I could explain to you, then, how I got to a point of using narcotics. It sounds so inhuman on paper.

So many days have lapsed. I've been pretty sick; I'm sorry not to have mailed this before. I'm going to a hospital in New York City today, but you can write me at the same address if you wish.

Pray for me please. I'm scared.

Yours truly,<br>Cheryl"

As this book went to press, Cheryl's condition was extremely critical and there was little hope for her survival. When I hear all the talk about the fun and the intrigue of marijuana and LSD, all I can remember are Cheryl's haunting words, *"I am a vegetable."*

In Haight Ashbury I asked a frail, nervous junkie what advice he would give to a young person who was considering the use of drugs. I repeat his answer:

"Don't do it! For some reason we young people are so hard headed and thick. The more people try to warn us, the more we want to do it. But you usually turn on in degrees. When I first met hip people they said, 'Looking hip isn't all of it; you have to start turning on.' So, I started smoking grass, taking pills, then dropping acid and shooting up different things. A lot of young people start this way. It's really bad. Don't start the route. Stay square or you'll end up like me."

Junkies start with marijuana.
Junkies become vegetables!

# the smuggies

# 11. the smuggies

"To get into the best society nowa-
days, one has either to feed people,
amuse people, or shock people."
Wilde

Let's talk about the "Smuggies."

A smuggie is someone who has more money than you do and lets you know it.

A smuggie is anyone with a charge account who brags about it.

A smuggie is the kid with the biggest, longest, sportiest brand new automobile, who speeds around the neighborhood and sticks his nose up.

A smuggie is one who is promptly accepted by the college of his choice and boasts about it.

"A teenage smuggie," said a girl, "is any girl who know she's absolutely beautiful and makes you feel ugly."

Other smuggies include: The fellow who is class president, sports idol, star in the school plays, the one who easily captures school honors—and never lets anyone forget it.

"Smuggery" describes the snobbery and preju-
dice of those who belong to sororities or fraternities and look down on non-members.

A smuggie is the opposite of a hippie. A smuggie is clean, well dressed and shaved. To put it plainly, he is absolutely smug about his life and everything he does.

Smuggies seek personal identification in ways much different than the hippies. If everyone is wearing long hair, smuggies wear it short. If others dress wild, smuggies dress straight. They despise fads and boast about being uninhibited and nonconforming.

The smuggies look with disdain on the drug scene and all the "hypes" mixed up in it. They look down their intellectual noses at those who are hopelessly addicted to narcotics and say, "Poor freaks, they just don't have the intelligence to make it. I'll never go that way. I'm different; I have a head on my shoulders."

They are self-reliant and say that anyone can lift himself by his own bootstraps just so they believe in something—Buddha, Krishna, Santa Claus or Jesus. Brain power is their god.

The smuggies, for the most part, come from the middle class. Their parents have good jobs and they live in nice homes. Most that I have met have been spoiled, sheltered and have a holier-than-thou attitude. They remind me that the Bible says, "Pride goes before destruction and a haughty spirit before a fall," because I've seen so many of them fall.

A smuggie never really shakes off his pride—even though he may become a hippie "strung out" on narcotics, diseased, broken in body and living like a zombie in a nowhere world. I have met numerous strung-out smuggies who refuse to make an honest appraisal of themselves and who will not admit they are ragged, lost and way out. They resurrect old dreams about the day they will finish college to become a lawyer or engineer. There is nothing quite so pitiful as a broken down smuggie who things he still has it.

I have personally counseled thousands of smuggies who are putting on a big front but who inwardly are phonies. In a recent interview, nineteen-year-old Renie told me what it's like to be a smuggie.

"I've been pampered, spoiled and sheltered all my life. I had private tutors—everything I ever wanted. As a result, I became an intellectual, snob so to speak, a bit of a psychopath. I suppose, because I was around grownups and never around kids my own age. I didn't get along with them anyway, because I felt superior towards kids my own age. They didn't care much for me either.

When I was fifteen I let loose and met some older kids. Because of my mental capability, I was at ease with the college kids who were nineteen and twenty. The group was called a 'sosh' group; they drank and had cars and boats. I started dating and going to their hangouts. By the time I was seventeen I was completely dissatisfied with my friends in high school. Last year, I met a bunch of kids in a 'rock' band and lost myself in that. I was always striving to be different. I never liked the same fads everyone else did. I went to school dressed in unusual fashions, vogue clothes, no makeup and I was self-conscious of my every move. The search for self-identity was very strong in me. I joined this band and found my identity because everyone in it 'dug' me. I sort of mothered the band, like they never made any arrangements without asking me. They would practice at my house. Their parents didn't know it, but they'd come over and we'd all drink and smoke. These kids had never heard of turning on by drugs and neither had I.

The Rolling Stones had something about their music that tore me up inside. I've found this is the way a lot of kids are getting off the path. It is with the music, because there is just something about the beat, the chords, the electronic guitar, the noise and the screaming. It's completely riotous and uninhibited and you can't help but let yourself go. Just a 'rock out', so to speak.

I was more interested in this music than in school or anything else. I would lock myself in my room and turn up the stereo full blast and beat around with sticks. Sometimes I would dance in front of a mirror and work out all kinds of contortions and movements. I found myself getting deep into the music.

A rumor started flying that members of the band were dope addicts. The double and triple meanings to the words, I found, were messages about homosexuality and turning on with drugs and other abnormal things. I began to see that the music and the sound was like forbidden fruit. When I found how bad it really was, I was already hooked by music.

I didn't want to be known as a 'teeny bopper' and I was fed up with the rules of society. I started to let myself go and went 'hip' in clothing. Formerly, I had bought the latest fashions.

I started out as a snob, became intrigued, went off-beat, and from then on I started dropping acid and taking speed balls. I became a junkie, went to fail, and life became a weird trip. I was a freaked out snob."

The world is faced with a sound revolution and the smuggies are part of it. They worship new "spiritual sounds." They are tuning into limitless noise. They exalt young, electronic composers whose passion gig is the exploration of sound. Filling the quarters of the mind with daisy chains of electronic "thingiees," this new sound is curiously savage, attacking the ears and jolting the torso. A square individual experiences a nervous agony because all the wrong notes are supposed to be the right ones—and that's hard to take.

Friday and Saturday nights thousands of smuggies head for the discotheques to turn on and tune in for an electronic high. With the lights flashing, the drums pounding, sound reverberates from every direction until it equals the thunder of a megaton bomb. They dance, wiggle and writhe and unashamedly indulge in music orgasms—after which they retire to their cosy apartments and consider themselves regenerated.

From a snobbish fraternity kid to a swinging discotheque "chick," I have labeled a host of people smuggies. If you want to pin me down on this, I say, A SMUGGIE IS ANY INDIVIDUAL WHO SAYS TO HIMSELF, "I'M GLAD I'M NOT LIKE OTHER PEOPLE."

Did you know smuggies are not new on the scene? Jesus, nineteen centuries ago, cut smuggies down to size when He told them this story:

> "Two men went up into the temple to pray, one a Pharisee and the other a tax collector. The Pharisee stood and prayed thus with himself, 'God, I thank thee that I am not like other men, extortioners, unjust, adulterers, or even like this tax collector. I fast twice a week, I give tithes of all that I get.' But the tax collector, standing afar off, would not even lift his eyes to heaven, but beat his breast, saying, 'God, be merciful to me a sinner!'
> I tell you, this man went down to his house justified rather than the other; for everyone who exalts himself will be humbled, but he who humbles himself will be exalted." (Luke 18:10-14 RSV)

Do you get the message?

A smuggie can turn honest and become straight if he's big enough to become little, and strong enough to become weak. But, I can tell you, from practical experience, that smuggies usually don't listen to preaching. The thing that really gets through to a smuggie is pain and sorrow. Wise old

Ben Franklin must have believed that too for he said, "After crosses and losses, men grow humbler and wiser."

the "squares"

# 12. the "squares"

> "He that hath no cross deserves no crown."
>
> Quarles

"SQUARES?"

Would you believe "goodniks?"

A square is actually a goodnik who is scorned because he is not hip on new fads and persists in being unworldly, unsophisticated, unenlightened and refuses to bop. He doesn't dig far-out music and refuses to develop rock and roll fever.

Squares do not demonstrate nor do they question every cultural, ethical, political and religious value of the day. Squares are conventional and conforming. They don't burn their draft cards and even wear service uniforms with pride. Squares are wheels who make the world go 'round.

Before we go any further, let me confess that I'm a square. I am not a member of the hot minority of the disenchanted. Sure, there are things about the establishment that I despise but I refuse to wig out. I realize that sinful men have offended God and I am going to give as much of myself as I can to bridge that gap between God and man.

Unlike the squares, runaways are looking for a God who will "do something now." They say the world is falling apart and we are headed toward a police state or anarchy. Young revolutionaries are being born by the minute. Sitting in barrooms, dressed in army fatigues, they plot sabotage and call for "freedom now" by swinging, not singing.

Squares face the same problems confronting the yippies. Yippies say, "Expose the system; force it to commit acts of open brutality. Hound the establishment by confronting it with its sins. Pelt the police with bottles of urine and bags of fecal matter. Shame your parents and the politicians and all the other squares." They look down upon parents as part of a dying order. The yippies stage their demonstrations in living color, having become masters of the media. These bubble-gum cheeked combatants with bell bottom trousers swagger before T.V. cameras with natural ease. Among them are the thin-faced, pallid coeds, the black power boys and floozy sweet boys in ballet tights and lace shirts.

The squares, however, prefer reality to rhetoric, deeds to demonstrations. They believe that persevering for good brings positive results. Squares are not afraid to face the shame of a cross. They, too, have seen a white light in their expanded consciousness but it is the reality of a personal experience with Christ.

Squares do not look upon religion as neuroticism. They don't blame God for their "sentence of life" but rather grasp life as an exciting opportunity for meaningful existence. Squares don't tongue lash or put down hippies and runaways. They have sympathy for kids whose only heroes are guys with guitars. Squares don't comprehend the violence of the peace movement. Squares refuse to blow their class and call the cops pigs and fascists. Squares are also interested in human justice and civil rights, but they refuse to parade their love to the hoopla of floodlights and the sensational press.

Squares become lonely too. They know what it mean to drink the cup of pain, to face nights of confusion and hours of isolation. This is the loneliest generation of all time, but how loneliness is faced and overcome is the difference between the squares and runaways. The runaways believe as Milton Camas did, " 'Tis only daylight that makes sin." So they sleep in the day, and in the night search for the light of meaningful relationship which will dispel the aching loneliness. They use drugs to fill the emptiness of their existence. Nights are spent in drunkenness, revelry and flipping out; days are spent in remorse and pain. Squares prefer to face their loneliness. They believe the solution is in "putting out, not wigging out."

By tuning in to others, they turn off their own problems. Being powered by the dynamo of God's love and care, they can soar above the common grind.

A square is not afraid of time; it is his friend, not his enemy. In time, God does reach the patient but desperate heart that seeks direction and meaning in life.

In 1968, while more than one million people ran away from home in the United States and Canada, more than 25 million squares preferred home. Though many prodigal sons wander aimlessly in the pig pens of perversion—millions of squares are purposefully laying foundations for freedom.

The boldest, bravest squares I know have been transformed by the power of God at our Teen Challenge Center. They are converted drug addicts, prostitutes, and alcoholics. These former runaways now are squares and proud of it.

Briefly let me tell you about one of our squares. Bob was brought up in a middle class home on Long Island and at twelve years of age, secretly began drinking hard liquor with his gang. When he was thirteen, he tried marijuana and when that novelty wore off he sniffed glue and that lead to goof balls. From there he went on to heroin and LSD. (He stole anything at home or elsewhere, to support his habit.) By the time he was 18, Bob had been on 25 LSD trips, his brain was damaged and he had served time in jail. Doctors, psychiatrists and group therapy did not help him.

In desperation, he came to Teen Challenge in Brooklyn where he was introduced to the power of God. That was the beginning of a miracle, for Bob found forgiveness through Christ and kicked his habit. His mind was healed and recently he expressed the desire to enter the ministry.

Bob is only one real life illustration of the many fellows and girls who have found purpose and meaning through faith in Christ. They enjoy being squares.

If being square means not taking drugs, not dressing in kooky clothes, not selling your body to the highest bidder nor running away from the responsibilities and problems of life, then I pray, God give us more squares!

*THINK SQUARE*

Able
Bright
Clean
Decent
Efficient
Faithful
Good
Honest
Industrious
Just
Kind
Loving
Mannerly
Noble
Obedient
Patriotic
Qualified
Respectful
Strong
Truthful
Understanding
Victorious
Worshiping
Exceptional
Yourself
Zealous

Think square and you'll never run in circles!

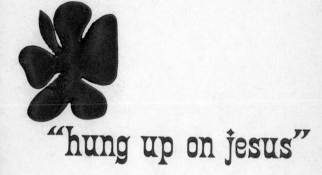

"hung up on jesus"

# 13. "hung up on jesus"

> "Men will wrangle for religion; write
> for it; fight for it; die for it; anything
> but live it."
>
> Colton

"Pop, I want to talk to you. Can you come up to
the apartment?"

Vic looked up and saw his son, Pete. Vic immediately sensed something urgent in the boy's voice
and it made him stop cold. Pete had never used
that tone of voice with him before. There had
always been excellent rapport between the two
even though the father had been a drug addict for
years. He loved his son so much he actually felt this
love would one day enable him to kick his drug
habit.

Vic climbed the stairs to the apartment and sat
down on the bed in his son's room.

"Pop, I'm *tired*. I'm so tired of you. You've made
so many promises but you will always be a drug
addict. You can never change, Pop. Why don't you
just go live in San Francisco or some place else far
away?"

Vic found it hard to believe what he was hear-
ing. His throat felt parched, and his heart began to
pound so fiercely he feared Pete could actually see
it. He was crushed—but being a strong man he

tried to hold back the tears which forced their way to the surface. Pete had never shown any sign of disgust, shame or disrespect toward his father before and this sudden outburst crushed Vic.

*Doesn't he know I've tried everything? He knows I've been to hospitals and to clinics and jails . . . I've tried, I've tried! I can't help myself,* cried Vic to himself.

Vic ran from the room. Overwhelmed by anguish, he wanted to be alone. He found a vacant lot and began to walk blindly in circles. Jerking his head to the sky he cried aloud:

"God, please God, help me! I don't know what to do. Take this monkey off my back. Set me free from this curse. Please help!"

Vic sobbed out his heart to God. He sat down and began thinking about his past life. It seemed only yesterday that Vic had been a sixteen-year-old-boy going to nightclubs, drinking, dancing and smoking marijuana. While many people say one cannot become addicted to marijuana, Vic knew he was psychologically addicted. When he tried to quit smoking pot, he was powerless to do so. It seemed that to have any fun at all he had to have it, even to listen to records or to make conversation. Nothing was fun without marijuana.

One day a friend said to him, "Look, Vic, you need something that will really make you fly. Take a sniff."

Vic took his first snort of heroin. He had opened the gates of hell and from that day on it was all downhill. He began to "skin pop" and finally he became a "mainliner", injecting heroin directly into his bloodstream. His life became a nightmare. His body became his enemy and he fed it only on heroin, alcohol and anything that caused him to forget.

Vic had voluntarily signed himself into the federal hospital for narcotics addicts in Lexington, Kentucky, and after fifty days his body was strong again and he felt fully recovered. He returned to his old neighborhood and had resolved only to drink and smoke marijuana ... no more heroin. But within three days he was shooting "stuff" into his veins again. He hated himself for doing it but he felt totally powerless to fight it.

Vic took a second "cure" at Lexington not long after this but it was the same story. Giving up hope, he gave himself over completely to a junkie's way of life for thirteen long years.

Vic's brother, Sammy, had been delivered from drugs and was a new man. Vic could never understand why he was not able to kick his habit as Sammy had. He remembered some of the weird things Sammy had told him. "Vic, you can't do it by yourself. Christ is your only hope! You've got to have God's help and His strength. Look at me! You saw how I was living and you know I had tried many times to kick my habit by myself. Just looking at me should convince you, Vic. Christ is your only hope!"

He was proud Sammy was clean; Sammy had found an answer to his problem but Vic could not accept it for himself. Several times he had attended church service with Sammy but still felt "religion" was not for him. But now as Vic thought back over the years, he decided to call Sammy and see if he would come help him. The words Sammy had told him kept going over and over in his mind, "Vic, Christ is your only hope ... your only hope ... only hope!"

Sammy was overjoyed to learn Vic was finally ready to give God a chance in his life. He clearly and lovingly explained once more the simple truth that Christ comes into a person's life to change it. Oh, the simplicity of it. Sammy led his brother to a new life in Christ. Finally Vic was ready to accept the truth for himself and apply it to his own life. He entered the Teen Challenge program and today he is one of our most faithful staff workers.

Vic's son, Pete, has been delighted by his father's deliverance from drugs. He is proud of his father and whenever Vic speaks of his son today his face glows with pride and joy.

"I see my son often and he has regained his respect for me. He is proud of me and although he has not accepted Christ, I am after him..." Vic told one of the other staff workers recently.

The greatest glow of all comes upon Vic's face, however, when he speaks of his Saviour. This quiet man possesses an inner strength and character of soul which comes from his radiant new faith.

"I love my Lord," he says often, "... and I'm 'hung up' on Jesus now."

Addicts, prostitutes, gangs, homosexuals and people with problems keep on getting "hung up" on Jesus at our Teen Challenge centers all around the world. How do they kick their habits? How do they become clean? What power is behind the miraculous changes? What kind of message do we preach to get this kind of results?

Here is our message to the runaway generation—to the hooked—the moral slave—the rootless rebel:

God did not create just worshiping robots who would exist as dull, uninteresting perfect beings. He created man free to make his own choices. God makes Himself known to man by means of a revelation, for God cannot appear to man as He is nor can He be understood by the senses. We must know someone before we can trust him, and that goes for God too. Apart from Christ, problems are never really solved. These Old Testament illustrations explain what I mean:

The story of Noah and his generation sounds as though it were written about our own day! The earth was corrupt and filled with violence. God said, "The end of all flesh is come before me, for the earth is full of wickedness through men, and behold, I will destroy them with the earth" (Genesis 6:13). God flooded the earth and everyone died, except those in the ark of old Noah, considered to be a "square" in his day. But was the problem of corruption, violence, drunkenness and illicit sex solved? Indeed not!

No sooner had Noah left the ark and planted vineyards, when "he drank of the vine, and was drunken, and he was uncovered (naked) in his tent" (Genesis 9:21). A son, Canaan, discovered his father's nudity and mocked him. Only one family was left on the earth and already drunkenness was a part of the scene.

Another example is Abraham, the best man of his generation. He had a real problem. His nephew and family lived in the doomed cities of Sodom and Gomorrah. Not even ten righteous men could be found in the two cities; sodomy, prostitution, rape and violence were rampant. In answer to Abraham's prayer the Lord saved Lot and his family before He rained fire and brimstone upon Sodom and Gomorrah. Lot was saved physically but not spiritually. The basic problem of the family was not solved, for, "Lot went up out of Zoar and dwelt in a mountain—his two daughters with him—and he dwelt in a cave." While Sodom still smoldered, the youngest daughter said, "Let us make our father drink wine, and we will lay with him that we may preserve the seed of our fathers." Here is a picture of drunkenness, incest and deception. Were the sins of Sodom any worse? Did the fire and the brimstone solve the sin problems? Obviously not!

These examples point out that there was no solution to the sin problem before Jesus Christ and His cross! Certainly God had given just laws by which man could govern life and its many problems, but man could not keep them because of his own weakness. Then Jesus came—sent by God into the world to deal once and for all with the sin problem that had plagued the human family from the beginning. Christ was commissioned and given the power to redeem lost mankind and what is more, to enter into the lives of people through the presence of His Holy Spirit. Christ is God's final and complete answer not only to the sin problem but to every problem in a person's life.

Hippies are right about one thing—life can be one big problem. That big problem is made up of a thousand little ones which are caused primarily by sin, our own flaws or weaknesses. I know that some call it "maladjustment" and even fancier names but we had better call it what God calls it and He clearly labels it as sin. Sin is rebellion against God and His laws; it is wanting to be boss of your own life and seeing no need to please God.

The Bible states, "All have sinned," and that includes the so-called moral "good guy" as well as the pagan "bad guys," the religious, as well as those without any religion. What everyone needs is a change of mind, heart and direction.

A person has two choices regarding his sin. He can do as many are—excuse himself and use the "big blame" argument: "I was made like this; I cannot help myself; my parents are to blame; my environment is to blame; God is to blame." Or a person can accept God's remedy for sin.

The Bible does not offer easy formulas or a set of automatic problem solvers. It offers something better than solutions to single situations. God offers *an ultimate solution. One that touches every problem in life.*

Jesus Christ is the *supreme answer and the only answer!* He makes the difference between your being bound or free, condemned or pardoned. He is the greatest manifestation of God's power and love on earth; the Head of the Universe and Source of all Wisdom, superceding all philosophy, ritual and law.

Contrary to what some claim, many outstanding men have accepted the facts of the Gospel and testify to the power of Christ. For example, Lambert Dolphin, Jr., Stanford University research physicist, says:

I wasn't even a true scientist until I met Jesus Christ. I couldn't be, for I was cut off from reality. Life with God is the only reality. And that is possible only through faith in Jesus Christ and His atoning death for our sins. Jesus Christ is the answer to the secret of the universe. In Him I've found the reason for life and the key to everything.

Walter F. Burke, as general manager of Project Mercury and Gemini, acknowledged: "I found nothing in science or space exploration to compel me to throw away my Bible or to reject my Saviour, Jesus Christ, in whom I trust."

We cannot fully comprehend how the death of Christ on the cross saves us, but we do know He paid our debt by dying there in our place. If we believe this, we are set free from the guilt and power of sin.

Accepting Christ, or putting faith in Him, not only gains full pardon and forgiveness but it also makes you a new person! This is not the end but the beginning of a new, thrilling life of faith in Jesus Christ. Christ comes not merely to affect your life, but to live it. He has the answers to your problems, doubts, perplexities—and you turn them all over to Him.

Accepting Jesus Christ as the ultimate solution to life's problems is only a part of it! Faith in Him will bring what most people really want out of life— inner joy, peace, love, hope, security, accomplishment, purpose—these are the deep cravings of everyone, expressed or unexpressed. Right relationship with God will bring right relationships with people. This is not a false idealism or escapism into a dream world—this is a reality.

I'm glad I'm hung up on Jesus.

You can be, too!

1. Confess to God and yourself that you are a sinner and be sorry for it.
2. Admit that you can't help yourself.
3. Accept Jesus Christ as the ultimate solution.
4. Read God's Word and obey it.
5. Take one step at a time by faith.
6. Share your faith with others.

## A BEGINNING PRAYER

Dear God, I will not try to kid myself any longer. I admit I have done things which I know to be terribly wrong. I'm a sinner and I'm sorry for all the things I've done to hurt You and others. Right now I'm at the end of my rope. I need Your help. I believe Christ died for me and I acknowledge Him as my Saviour from sin, and my guide through life. Give me Your Holy Spirit in great measure. Help me to live moment by moment in Your love and care. Give me strength to share Your love with others. In Jesus' name, I pray. Amen.